PRAISE FOR *TONI MORRISON'S SPIRITUAL VISION*

"Nadra Nittle has written just the book we need: an engaging and thorough consideration of Toni Morrison's religious vision. For too long Morrison's significant spiritual influence has been unspoken or, at best, misunderstood. No more. Nittle skillfully journeys through the novelist's life, fiction, and faith and retains Morrison's paradoxes while offering readers essential truths: 'Catholicism . . . did not exist in the margins of Morrison's life,' she writes. Nittle concludes that Morrison 'told the public what she thought they should know: she was a Catholic, she took matters of faith seriously, and that wasn't up for debate'—and shows an expert understanding of the novelist's sensibility."

—Nick Ripatrazone, author of *Longing for an Absent God*

"In Nadra Nittle's *Toni Morrison's Spiritual Vision*, the author masterfully details the myriad ways Morrison weaved religion, spirituality, and African and African American folklore into her stories. Nittle's book is a wonderful exploration of how Morrison combined her religious background, including her Catholic faith, with the African American tradition (dating back to the African tradition) of storytelling. Exploring common themes throughout Morrison's work, this book is a must-have for fans who want a deeper dive into what made the late writer's stories so compellingly magical."

—Del Sandeen, author of *Maya Angelou: Writer and Activist*

"In this lively study, Nadra Nittle presides over religion, history, culture, and literary aesthetics to bring to us nothing less than the Gospel according to Toni Morrison. Elements of Black history, African folklore, theology, classical mythology, and biblical typology gather at the seams of Morrison's spiritual cosmogeny. The communities populating her gothic landscapes transcend moral history. In the transhistorical sweep of the story Nittle tells, the living struggle, falter, and rise only to find that destiny is rarely appointed. And redemption in Morrison's alternative economy of salvation is a quasi-autonomous quest for the many lives and many selves that make up an American selfhood. Integrating disciplines and genres, this suggestive work will garner a wide readership. Morrison fans will cheer its journalistic eloquence, archival analysis, and provocative payoffs and, most of all, its unfolding revelations of a Nobel laureate in the making."

—Gregory S. Jackson, Rutgers University, author of
The Word and Its Witness: The Spiritualization of American Realism

"*Toni Morrison's Spiritual Vision: Faith, Folktales, and Feminism in Her Life and Literature* is the seminal text for anyone who wants to gain a deeper understanding of an underappreciated yet central part of Morrison's life and literature: her Catholic faith."

—Ekemini Uwan, public theologian
and cohost of *Truth's Table* podcast

TONI MORRISON'S
SPIRITUAL VISION

FAITH, FOLKTALES, AND
FEMINISM IN HER LIFE
AND LITERATURE

TONI MORRISON'S SPIRITUAL VISION

FAITH, FOLKTALES, AND
FEMINISM IN HER LIFE
AND LITERATURE

NADRA NITTLE

FORTRESS PRESS
MINNEAPOLIS

TONI MORRISON'S SPIRITUAL VISION
Faith, Folktales, and Feminism in Her Life and Literature

Cover image: © Getty Image 2021; Toni Morrison, Paris Match, Issue 3302 by Sebastien Micke/Contour. Cover design: Lindsey Owens

Print ISBN: 978-1-5064-7151-8
eBook ISBN: 978-1-5064-7152-5

Contents

1

Black, Christian, and Feminist

Toni Morrison's Village Literature

"Invisible to whom? Not to me."[1]

Toni Morrison once made this quip about Ralph Ellison's 1952 novel *Invisible Man* to distinguish herself from the Black male writers who came before her. She suspected that authors such as Ellison, Richard Wright, and James Baldwin—who described his inner critic as the "little white man deep inside of all of us"[2]—wrote books with white readers in mind. Morrison pointed out that while white people appear in her books, she crafted her novels without "having the white critic sit on your shoulder and approve it."[3] Instead, Morrison wrote her books first and foremost for Black people, a choice for which she refused to apologize. Just as Tolstoy wrote for a Russian audience, she explained, she was writing for Black readers—many of whom have remained devoted fans beyond her death at age eighty-eight in 2019.

Her decision to approach literature through an African American lens meant writing books rooted in the Black oral tradition whereby storytelling is not an individual endeavor but a group effort that mirrors the communal nature of Black life throughout the African diaspora. Morrison wrote what she characterized as "village literature, fiction that is really for the village, for the tribe,"[4] and, in this way, her fiction includes all the complexities of the village experience. Rather than stick to the point, her narrators sometimes veer off course, only to return to the topic at hand after an aside, much like village storytellers do—a tradition this book will follow. Also, her novels aren't just told from one point of view but from the multiple perspectives found in any group or tribe.

The speech patterns of her characters originate from African American culture, specifically those of her family members. Born Chloe Ardelia Wofford in 1931 in the ethnically diverse steel town of Lorain, Ohio, Morrison grew up hearing the stories of Mexican, Italian, and Greek immigrants, often marveling at them. But nothing topped how fluidly her relatives used language,[5] and she wanted her fiction to reflect their verbal dexterity.

"When something terribly important was to be said, it was highly sermonic, highly formalized, biblical in a sense, and easily so," Morrison recalled of her family. "They could move easily into the language of the King James Bible and then back to standard English, and then segue into language that we would call 'street.'"[6]

Morrison's family took pride in the fact that her grandfather read the Bible five times from cover to cover.[7] With reading materials limited—"there were no books, no libraries"—the Bible was the only book available to him, and his decision to read the Scriptures amounted to "taking power back," since it had been illegal for enslaved African Americans to read. Following her grandfather's example, Morrison's parents had books throughout their household. "That was like resistance," she said, but the Bible remained the family's literary foundation.

At the core of Morrison's literature is the Black community, and at the heart of that is African American religion, as it was in her family. Black America regarded Christianity as a belief system of liberation and wed it with West African oral, spiritual, and folk traditions. This religious sensibility shapes the stories Morrison chose to tell, how she told them, and the characters within them. In her effort to capture how the African Americans she knew conversed, worshipped, healed, loved, and told their own stories, Morrison created a literary universe in which the supernatural and the church coexist with the dual horrors of racial oppression and misogyny. Her engagement of the spiritual world allowed Morrison to center Black characters, particularly women, whose otherworldly gifts empower them in a society determined to strip them of their agency.

She wrote novels, she said, that reflect the shrewd decisions Black people make to survive, all while experiencing "some great supernatural element."[8] In her books, as in life, faith in the invisible—be it in God or magic—"make[s] the world larger"[9] for African Americans.

The Black Church's Effect on Black Storytellers

The fact that the Bible influenced the speech of Morrison's relatives (and, later, her literature) wasn't at all unusual. Across time, this was the norm for African Americans, as evidenced by the Black church's effect on the storytelling styles of the late James Baldwin, Morrison's contemporary, and President Barack Obama, three decades her junior. Born seven years before Morrison and raised in neighboring New York, Baldwin said that serving as a teen pastor in his father's Fireside Pentecostal Assembly Church in Harlem shaped both his personal character and the cadence of his language—from his melodious use of words to his talent for scene setting.

Recalling his adolescence, Baldwin said, "Those three years in the pulpit—I didn't realize it then—that is what turned me into a writer, really, dealing with all that anguish and that despair and that beauty."[10]

More recently, the speeches of Barack Obama have drawn comparisons to sermons. The forty-fourth president has routinely invoked both Jesus and the Sermon on the Mount in his talks and broke into a rendition of "Amazing Grace" while eulogizing the victims of a 2015 hate crime at Mother Emanuel Church in Charleston, South Carolina. The son of a white Kansan mother and a Black Kenyan father, Obama grew up in Hawaii and Indonesia removed from the African American church, but after moving to the continental United States and converting to Christianity as an adult, he attended Trinity United

Church of Christ on Chicago's predominantly Black South Side. There, he absorbed the Black sermonic style, complete with the call-and-response tradition in which a pastor shouts out a line, and the congregation—or as Morrison might put it, the "village"—replies. With African origins, call-and-response continues to mold Black speech and literature centuries after the first Africans landed in the Americas in chains. The tradition is found throughout Morrison's oeuvre, notably in a pivotal church scene in *Song of Solomon* (1977).

Along with religious allusions, Obama has peppered his speech with street language and colloquialisms akin to how Morrison's family members did and her fictional characters do. Addressing a heavily Black crowd in South Carolina while campaigning for president, he used African American Vernacular English (AAVE) and slang to object to how his rivals were deceiving the public about his policy stances and religious beliefs.

"They're trying to bamboozle you," he said in January 2008. "It's the same old okey-doke. Y'all know about the okey-doke, right?"[11] He went on to say "hoodwink," which along with "bamboozle" was a word Nation of Islam leader Malcolm X famously used. To quash the smear that he was a Muslim, Obama pointed out how he'd been a member of the same church for twenty years, "prayin' to Jesus *wit'* my Bible."[12]

He never explicitly referred to racism during his speech, but the use of AAVE and colloquialisms largely associated with Malcolm X made his intentions clear to the African Americans in the crowd. This is known as signifying, which sociologist Michael Eric Dyson defines as the Black tradition of "hinting at ideas or meanings veiled to outsiders."[13] According to Dyson, "Obama's risky move played to inside-group understanding even as he campaigned in the white mainstream: denying he was Muslim, he fastened onto the rhetoric of the most revered Black Muslim, beat for beat."[14] Morrison's literature is filled with signifying—her books include cultural references, turns of phrase, and traditions that may not register to readers who aren't African American.

In a different 2008 campaign speech, Obama motioned as if he was brushing off his "haters," a nod to rapper Jay-Z's 2003 hit "Dirt off Your Shoulder." After this gesture, he drew cheers from the crowd in the same way theatrical Black preachers elicit praise from church members, which Morrison captures in novels such as *Sula* (1973). The idea of brushing dirt off one's shoulder may very well be rooted in Jesus Christ's advice to his disciples to "shake the dust off [their] feet"[15] should anyone not welcome them into their homes or listen to their message. In Black culture, even hip-hop expressions sometimes derive from Scripture.

Given the outsized influence of the Black church on Black language, Morrison's desire to write literature that "was irrevocably, indisputably Black,"[16] as she phrased it, went hand in hand with writing fiction that was inherently Christian. She said the religion appealed to African Americans on a psychic level because it offered a message of transcendent love, and Black people, of course, have survived unimaginable hatred. Today, as Americans grow increasingly less religious, 79 percent of Black people still identify as Christian,[17] a higher percentage than whites (70 percent) and Latinos (77 percent).

When discussing the historic importance of Christianity to the Black community, scholars tend to cite the Old Testament, noting that enslaved African Americans identified with the enslaved Israelites that Moses freed from Egypt in the book of Exodus. For liberating dozens of Black people from bondage, the abolitionist Harriet Tubman was famously nicknamed Moses, connecting the Israelite experience to the African American one.

Black women specifically have identified with Hagar in the book of Genesis. Forced into surrogate motherhood by Abraham and Sarah, the couple who enslaves her, Hagar and her son, Ishmael, are ultimately cast aside and take flight in the wilderness. Held captive during slavery and employed as maids during Jim Crow, African American women could relate to Hagar, for they, too, suffered sexual exploitation and served as substitute mothers to the white children they waited on, watched over, and wet-nursed. Morrison understood why Black people saw themselves in the Old Testament and named one of the characters in her 1977 novel *Song of Solomon* after Hagar. Yet she also noted that the New Testament resonated with African Americans and with her personally.

"The Bible wasn't part of my reading: It was part of my life," she said during a 1981 interview with author Charles Ruas. "The New Testament is so pertinent to Black literature—the lamb, the victim, the vulnerable one who does die but nevertheless lives."[18]

In many of her books, including *Sula*, *Song of Solomon*, and *Beloved* (1987), characters live on in some form despite dying. In *Beloved*, the infant slain by her mother to avoid a life of enslavement rises from the dead to exact her vengeance. In *Song of Solomon*, characters fly despite jumping to their deaths, and in *Sula*, the woman blamed for the evil in her village dies painlessly but lives on to relish that fact. In the novels of Toni Morrison, death isn't the end of one's journey because African Americans, grounded in their Christian faith, have not believed that death equals an absolute end. The 1934 film *Imitation of Life*, based on Fannie Hurst's novel of the same name, is a case in point and directly influenced Morrison. It follows Delilah Johnson, a Black mother with a striving daughter named Peola who is pale enough to pass for white and abandons her mother to cross the color line.

Marginalized in a racially stratified society that leads her own child to reject her, Delilah fixates on life after death, saving nearly all of her meager earnings for an elaborate funeral. The white characters in the film find her seeming preoccupation with death morbid; Delilah, however, isn't focusing on death but on the afterlife. Unlike the enslaved Africans who, lore says, didn't jump to their deaths but flew away to liberate themselves from bondage, Delilah doesn't actively cause her own demise. Still, she remains steadfast that she'll receive the dignity that eludes her in life in the hereafter.

Morrison alludes to *Imitation of Life* in her debut novel, *The Bluest Eye* (1970), in which a Black father rapes and impregnates his young daughter. With a slight tweak, she names the book's tragic little girl character, Pecola, after the film's "tragic mulatto" character, Peola. While the dark-skinned Pecola longs for blue eyes, the light-skinned Peola is willing to turn away a loving mother for would-be acceptance in a white supremacist society that loathes Blackness.

"Black women have . . . been given . . . the cross," Morrison said of her first book. "They don't walk near it. They're often on it. And they've borne that, I think, extremely well."[19]

Hence the Christianity in Morrison's literature isn't just uniquely Black but includes the divine feminine. It is entangled with African folklore and mythology; unorthodox preaching based on biblical principles and community mores; and women's healing, power, and intuition. Her books engage religious syncretism, or the blending of discrete faith and folk traditions, because enslavement forced Black people throughout the diaspora to meld the religious beliefs of their captors with African customs and spiritual practices, giving rise to new strains of Christianity.

Black Liberation Theology

With a mother who belonged to the African Methodist Episcopal (AME) Church, a denomination where race and religion intersected from the outset, Morrison grew up understanding Black Christianity as a philosophy of refuge, if not liberation, for African Americans.

The first Protestant denomination established by African Americans, the AME Church was formally recognized in 1816, but its origins date back to the late 1700s, when white officials at St. George's Methodist Episcopal Church ousted a group of Black worshippers from the sanctuary in an act of racial animus.[20] The incident made the leaders of the Free African Society (FAS), a Philadelphia organization that held religious services and provided mutual aid for free people of color and their descendants, determined to form their own church.

Made up of Black Methodists and Episcopalians, Bethel AME Church started in 1794, with FAS leader Richard Allen as pastor. The formerly enslaved Allen wanted his new church to be autonomous to prevent meddling from white Methodists, so he sued in the Pennsylvania courts in 1807 and 1815 to give his church the right to be independent. After this successful legal fight, Allen invited other African Americans seeking religious autonomy to join him in forming a new Wesleyan Methodist Church denomination that would be known as the African Methodist Episcopal Church.

By the 1850s, AME churches could be found across the country—including California, New York, and Morrison's Ohio. Three decades later, the denomination swelled to four hundred thousand people thanks to members proselytizing to newly freed people of color during the Civil War and Reconstruction. Once the 1890s arrived, the church spread to the West African countries of Liberia and Sierra Leone.

The AME Church follows Methodist doctrine, but its focus on racial issues distinguishes it from the Wesleyan Methodist Church. Historically and today, AME leaders have emphasized the Black presence in Christianity's origins. For example, Bishop Benjamin T. Tanner wrote in the 1895 book *The Color of Solomon* that scholars had inaccurately portrayed Jesus as a white man, and twenty-first-century researchers have largely confirmed his assertion. AME leaders have criticized not only Eurocentric Christianity but also churches, Black and white alike, for failing to adequately address race, class, and gender oppression.

In this Black-affirming religious environment, Toni Morrison spent her formative years, though she associated the AME Church more with her mother than with the denomination's progressive racial ideology. "In my mother's church, everybody read the Bible, and it was mostly about music," she recalled during a 2016 National Public Radio (NPR) interview. "My mother had the most beautiful voice I have ever heard in my life. She could sing anything—classical, jazz, blues, opera. And people came from long distances to . . . the A.M.E. church she belonged to just hear her. So, for me, her church was about her and music—the choir and her brilliant, wonderful solos. The lessons, you know, were like fairytales to me."[21]

As a child, Morrison said, she "was perfectly content"[22] with the aesthetics of religion but grew more serious about her faith as she aged. She converted to Catholicism at twelve, baptized her two sons when she became a mother, and included the principles of Black liberation theology—popularized by AME pastor James H. Cone—in her fiction.

During the civil rights movement of the 1960s, when African Americans demanded equal rights after decades of degradation via Jim Crow, Cone developed the principles of Black liberation theology. This theology examines the Christian Gospels from the perspective of society's most economically and racially disadvantaged groups, just as Jesus preached in the Gospel of Matthew that the "last shall be first, and the first last."[23] Drawn to the militancy of Black Muslim leaders like Malcolm X, some African Americans began to reject Christianity as the "white man's religion," but Cone challenged this notion.

"'No! The Christian Gospel is not the white man's religion," he said. "It is a religion of liberation, a religion that says God created all people to be free. But I realized that for Black people to be free, they must first love their blackness."[24]

This revelation prompted Cone to evaluate the racism rampant in the country's economic and criminal justice systems. Black liberation theology, he said, coupled the Reverend Martin Luther King Jr.'s Christian viewpoints with Malcolm X's radical love of Blackness. By 1969, Cone's book *Black Theology & Black Power* debuted and is now regarded as Black liberation theology's foundational text. Through his work, he aimed "to speak on behalf of the voiceless Black masses in the name of Jesus, whose Gospel I believed had been greatly distorted by the preaching theology of white churches."[25]

In 2018, the year of his death, Cone won the Grawemeyer Award in Religion for his book *The Cross and the Lynching Tree*, which compared the crucifixion of Jesus to the lynching of African Americans, very much analogous to how Morrison explores the persecution of Black women and girls in her novels. As a Catholic, however, the principles of Catholic liberation theology informed her worldview as well. Like Black liberation theology, this branch of the movement—started by Peruvian theologian

Gustavo Gutiérrez—dates back to the mid-twentieth century and posits that the church must do more than empathize with and serve the poor; rather, it must fight against the systemic inequality responsible for poverty and other forms of oppression. Catholic liberation theology influenced supporters to take part in Latin American political uprisings, such as the 1979 Sandinista revolt against Anastasio Somoza Debayle's dictatorship in Nicaragua and the 1964 formation of the Ejército de Liberación Nacional (National Liberation Army) in Colombia.

But the Catholic liberation theology of Gutiérrez, whom Cone greatly admired, did not speak to the Black American experience. Moreover, Black liberation theology focused more on Black manhood than womanhood, leading two of Cone's Black women students, Jacquelyn Grant and Delores Williams, to pioneer what's now known as womanist theology. Also called womanist Christology, it interprets the Gospels through the Black female perspective.

"Christ among the least must also mean Christ in the community of Black women,"[26] explained Grant, author of *White Women's Christ and Black Women's Jesus: Feminist Christology and Womanist Response.* This philosophy forms the backbone of Morrison's writing, as she was equally likely to explore the crucifixion, or victimization, of Black women in her works as she was their divinity, a pattern that started with *The Bluest Eye.*

"When I began, there was just one thing that I wanted to write about, which was the true devastation of racism on the most vulnerable, the most helpless unit in the society—a black female and a child," Morrison said.[27]

To understand womanist theology, it's first necessary to grasp the meaning of the term *womanist* and its significance to Black women. Coined by writer Alice Walker, the term *womanist* derives from the AAVE expression "You acting womanish,"[28] which Black mothers in the first half of the twentieth century might have told daughters who displayed "outrageous, audacious, courageous or willful behavior" or wanted "to know more and in greater depth than is considered 'good' for one." More recently, Black mothers might tell such children that they're "acting grown."

In her 1983 book *In Search of Our Mothers' Gardens: Womanist Prose*, Walker defines the term *womanist*, in part, as a Black feminist or a feminist of color who appreciates women's culture and strength and is "committed to survival and wholeness of entire people, male *and* female."[29] A womanist can love women or men sexually or nonsexually and, therefore, is not a "gender separatist." Womanists are also universalists, meaning they recognize that Blackness comes in all shades, just like the flowers in a flower garden do. They love "the struggle," "the folk," and themselves, regardless of the triple oppression they face in the forms of race, class, and gender. Due to the multifaceted nature of womanism, Walker viewed it as richer than the white feminist tradition, using the analogy that "womanist is to feminist as purple is to lavender."[30]

Walker left room for a religious dimension in her description of womanists, characterizing these women as lovers of the moon and the spirit. Womanists define spirituality on their own terms but share the common goal of using their connection to spirit to improve the lives of their families, their communities, and themselves. While womanists are often dedicated churchgoers, their spirituality transcends the institution of Christianity. They might turn to the Bible for guidance, but they also draw on folk traditions and their own spiritual gifts—be it psychic visions, healing powers, or their relationships with God, nature, and their ancestors—for insight.

Although Morrison didn't define her literature as womanist or feminist—"I don't write 'ist' novels,"[31] she said—she acknowledged the womanist movement. "Womanists is what Black feminists used to call themselves," she told *Interview* magazine in 2012. "They were not the same thing. And, also, the relationship with men. Historically, Black women have always sheltered their men because they were out there, and they were the ones that were most likely to be killed."[32]

The Black women characters in Morrison's books may not identify as womanists, but discovering the divinity within themselves gives them meaning in life and value in their communities. They find empowerment through an eclectic mix of spiritual practices that are equal parts American and African, Christian and pagan. Such women first appear in *The Bluest Eye* and continue to turn up throughout Morrison's literary catalog.

The Bluest Eye as the Blueprint

When Toni Morrison wrote *The Bluest Eye*, she didn't yet consider herself a writer and, thus, didn't know that the themes in this devastating novel about a girl traumatized by the colorism, anti-Blackness, and dysfunction of her family and community would inform each of her subsequent books. But *The Bluest Eye* was, in many ways, the blueprint for Morrison's body of work. As it chronicles Pecola Breedlove's trauma, it also explores the roles that faith, magic, the village, wisewomen, and folklore play in African American culture.

"If my work is to confront a reality unlike that received reality of the West, it must centralize and animate information discredited by the West—discredited not because it is not true or useful or even of some racial value, but because it is information held by discredited people, information dismissed as 'lore' or 'gossip' or 'magic' or 'sentiment,'" Morrison explained in her 1984 essay "Memory, Creation, and Writing."[33]

The West may have discredited the customs of the Africans it enslaved and dehumanized, but in *The Bluest Eye*, Morrison illustrates how Western culture, particularly white American culture, is not only oppressive but also filled with "lore" and "magic" of its own. The book begins with a riff on the Dick and Jane characters featured in the basal reader series that helped an estimated eighty-five million US schoolchildren learn to read from the 1930s to the 1960s.[34] *The Bluest Eye* opens, "Here is the house. It is green and white. It has a red door. It is very pretty. Here is the family. Mother, Father, Dick, and Jane. They are very happy."[35]

As the passage continues, the reader detects that something is awry in this family. Neither Father nor Mother plays with Jane, and neither pet plays with her either. In this distorted version of Dick and Jane (eventually the repetitive lines all run together sans punctuation), the daughter of the family is isolated, as is Pecola Breedlove in her household. This is not the Dick and Jane taught so widely in US schools that the characters and story lines have essentially become American folklore. Rather, the story that unfolds about the Breedlove family is the truth about the catastrophic impact of racial oppression on one Black household.

In the Dick and Jane universe, racism, poverty, and, certainly, child rape do not exist. The family, after all, is "very happy." But the characters made their debut during a time when most American families, Black or white, were in turmoil due to the Great Depression. Suicides reportedly rose from 17 per 100,000 people in 1929 to 21.3 per 100,000 people in 1932.[36] And unlike Dick and Jane's businessman father, men were out of work, and women couldn't count on their husbands to be the sole providers while they served as homemakers. For African American families— who often needed two providers, even when the economy was stable, to make it financially—the example of the breadwinner husband and the housewife never rang true. This model also didn't apply to Zerna Sharp, the Indiana schoolteacher who conceived of the series. Sharp worked outside the home and never became a wife or a mother, referring to Dick and Jane as "my children."[37] These characters and their unattainable lifestyles were utter fiction for many, but the impact of such a family, particularly on little Black girls like Pecola Breedlove, was very real. Although Pecola is also fictional, her character was inspired by a real-life Black girl Morrison once knew who craved blue eyes.

Pecola figures that if she had blue eyes (as Jane does), people would love her. But because of her dark eyes and skin, no one does. She is more than unloved; she is loathed. Even her own mother, who is not a homemaker but a maid for a white family, withholds affection from her and instead lavishes her attention on the Jane of that household.

While Pecola idolizes the Shirley Temples of the world and the "blue-eyed, yellow-haired, pink-skinned doll[s]" that represent them, her friend Claudia rejects the idea that white girls are superior. She dismembers the white dolls given to her in hopes of discovering "the secret of the magic they weaved on others." Claudia refuses to internalize anti-Black racism like the African Americans around her have. She doesn't view herself—and by extension, her Blackness—as the problem. Just as the Western world has discredited African customs as "lore" and "magic," Claudia disbelieves the mythology about white beauty.

But she and her sister, Freida, do believe in their "own magic." To their disappointment, no marigolds grew in their Ohio town in the fall of 1941. The girls believed if they "had planted the seeds, and said the right words over them, everything would be all right." In the end, not only does their spell fail, but their friend Pecola is pregnant with her father's child, to boot. Nothing would ever be all right for Pecola or Cholly Breedlove, her rapist father.

As the narrator revisits Cholly's early years, the reader learns that he, too, had a tragic childhood. His great-aunt Jimmy raises him after foiling his mother's attempt to leave him "on a junk heap by the railroad" when he was a newborn. She relishes her role as Cholly's savior but ignores how traumatic it might be for a child to hear that his mother discarded him like trash or that his father was never in the picture. His aunt gives him food and shelter but doesn't know how to nurture him emotionally. Through Jimmy, however, Cholly is introduced to the folk medicine that African Americans traditionally embraced, the wisewomen they relied on for their health, and the village women who form the backbone of the Black community.

Aunt Jimmy wears an asafetida bag around her neck, a practice African Americans adopted during slavery.[38] A gum resin from the roots of the Ferula asafetida plant, this herbal medicine was thought to prevent a variety of illnesses, including whooping cough, hysteria, diphtheria, smallpox, and measles. Twenty-first-century research studies have found that the plant has antioxidant, antiviral, antifungal, antidiabetic, and cancer chemopreventive properties, among others.[39] This underscores Morrison's point that the West did not have a valid reason to discredit African American customs as inferior. Westerners dismissed Black traditions as "rawness and savagery"[40]—as she argues in her book *Playing in the Dark: Whiteness and the Literary Imagination*—to provide "the staging ground and the arena for the quintessential American identity," such as the lore that is Dick and Jane.[41]

Although asafetida is a powerful herb, wearing it doesn't stop Jimmy from falling ill after she attends an outdoor church service following a rainstorm. "The damp wood of the benches was bad for her," causing her to feel "poorly" five days later.[42] When Jimmy's health suffers, the village women take action—making her chamomile tea, rubbing her with liniment, and reading the Bible to her. They also give her advice: "Don't eat no whites of eggs." "Drink new milk." "Chew on this root."[43] Jimmy ignores it all except for her friend Miss Alice's Bible reading. The words from First Corinthians emotionally comfort her, but they don't physically heal her, so the women decide to call upon the village healer, M'Dear. She is a midwife, a diagnostician, and the go-to person for "any illness that could not be handled by ordinary means—known cures, intuition, or endurance."[44]

To highlight how distinct this woman is from the rest of the village, the narrator mentions how M'Dear is a quiet woman who lives apart from the community in a shack near the woods, an image that conjures up the figures in the Bible who took refuge in the wilderness—from Hagar in the Old Testament to John the Baptist in the New Testament. The physical description of M'Dear is also reminiscent of the Bible. Cholly Breedlove has never met her before but expects M'Dear to be a shriveled-up and hunched-over old woman. Instead, M'Dear stands well over six feet tall, much taller than the preacher who accompanies her to visit the ailing Aunt Jimmy. Cholly is amazed by her stature, similar to how people in the Bible react when they encounter enormous angels who reassure them by saying, "Do not be afraid."[45] Of indeterminable age with an intimidating physique and the ability to cure the most confounding medical conditions, M'Dear is no mere woman but a sort of goddess. The fact that she towers above the village preacher and that the Scriptures don't heal Jimmy signals that Western Christianity alone won't suffice for African Americans. To get results, they must combine their religion with their folk customs and healing practices.

M'Dear diagnoses Jimmy, in part, by using her hickory stick as a divination tool. She taps it on the floor while examining her patient's wrinkled face. She then twists the knob with her right thumb while running her left thumb over Jimmy's body. After touching Jimmy's cheek and forehead and examining the sick woman's scalp, fingernails, back, and palm, M'Dear listens to her chest and stomach and takes a look at her stools, ordering the caregivers to bury them. Tapping her hickory stick, M'Dear offers her diagnosis and remedy to Jimmy: "You done caught cold in your womb. Drink pot liquor and nothing else."[46]

Packed with iron and vitamins C, K, and A, pot liquor is the juice left over from cooking greens and beans. African Americans and Southerners have traditionally imbibed it for its health benefits, and the village women don't hesitate to give Jimmy their pot liquor from turnip, collard, and mustard greens; beets; green beans; black-eyed peas; and a hog jowl. In just two nights, Jimmy regains much of her strength, but before she fully recovers, she eats a piece of peach cobbler that an acquaintance leaves for her. The next morning, Cholly finds her dead.

Aunt Jimmy may have perished, but the community doesn't really view her death as the end for her. While they are stunned by God's mysterious ways, they also take "joy in the termination of [Jimmy's] misery."[47] Since she had never been married, the village women stitch together a white wedding dress for her to wear to meet Jesus, whom Cholly perceives as white. "God was a nice old white man," he tells himself, "with long white hair, flowing white beard, and little blue eyes that looked sad when people died and mean when they were bad."[48]

But this limited view of God causes him to ignore the godliness of the African Americans in his life. When he wonders if God looks like a powerful Black father he encounters, a man whose "big arms looked taller than trees," Cholly quickly brushes aside the thought because God just has to be a white man. Later, he is so in awe of M'Dear that he dreams about her, but Cholly overlooks her holiness as well. Most tragically, Cholly fails to see how Christlike his own daughter is.

She's deemed ugly, just as Jesus was, a characteristic of Christ that has long been overlooked in artistic and cinematic depictions of his life. According to Isaiah 53:2, "He had no beauty or majesty to attract us to him, nothing in his appearance that we should desire him." Jesus didn't need to be beautiful, the Bible says, because "people look at the outward appearance, but the Lord looks at the heart."[49] And Pecola's heart contained "all one could expect of Jesus,"[50] Rondrea Danielle Mathis asserts in "She Shall Not Be Moved: Black Women's Spiritual Practice in Toni Morrison's *The Bluest Eye, Beloved, Paradise,* and *Home.*" She argues that Pecola "was loving, caring, benevolent, and kind, but no one can recognize her as a savior because she is Black; she is 'nothing to see.'"[51]

Suffering from internalized racism that makes them view Pecola's dark skin as ugly, the child's family and community reject her like humanity rejected and crucified Jesus Christ. Through Pecola, who has a mental breakdown after her rape and pregnancy, Morrison shows how Black girls and women "have been given the cross."[52] But through M'Dear, she shows how they have also "borne that extremely well."[53] The womanist Christology in *The Bluest Eye* instructs the reader to see both the vulnerability of Black women and girls and their inherent divinity. Black women may be horribly devalued in a country that ranks women of color at the bottom of the social hierarchy, but "God is no respecter of persons."[54] He values the Pecola Breedloves of the world as much as he does the Shirley Temples and the Dicks and Janes.

In Morrison's worldview, as in Christianity, the last do come first. This means Blackness and femaleness are not to be loathed but revered. Toni Morrison grew up convinced of this fact because the African Americans in her family weren't just faithful people. They appeared to her in many ways to be magical, to be divine.

The women in her family could interpret dreams, predict the future, and see ghosts, she said, but they were also faithful Christians and masterful storytellers who passed down African American folklore and folk traditions to her. In some capacity, each of her novels examines the themes of her upbringing—faith, folktales, and feminism. Like her powerful women characters, Morrison would distance herself from institutional religion to take an unstructured approach to spirituality that she largely kept private, but the Catholic and Protestant influences in her work are as evident as those rooted in African American customs. At a time when Americans are increasingly identifying as "spiritual but not religious" and exploring the faith traditions of their ancestors, Morrison's spiritual vision is more relevant than ever.

2

A Magical Black Heritage

Toni Morrison came very close to writing a memoir. Speaking at Ohio's Oberlin College in 2012 near her hometown of Lorain, she admitted that she'd gone so far as to sign an agreement with her publisher to write her life story, but later, she had second thoughts that prompted her to cancel the contract. "There's a point at which your life is not interesting, at least to me," she explained. "I'd rather write fiction."[1]

Life in Lorain

Certainly, Morrison's life wasn't as tragic or unfathomable as some of her characters' lives were. She grew up the second of four children in a two-parent home in a Midwestern town that, to an extent, spared her from the indignities of racial segregation. One high school yearbook photo of Morrison shows her with perfectly coiffed hair, a short-sleeved sweater, and a pencil skirt posing next to three white classmates, two of whom are draped in the letterman's cardigans of that era. Well-groomed and photogenic, Morrison and her peers look like they could be in an advertisement for the teenyboppers of the time. An attractive student who served as senior class treasurer and belonged to the debate team, the yearbook staff, and the drama club, Morrison's life didn't resemble Pecola Breedlove's in the slightest. Plus, she possessed an intellect that her teachers praised. Her junior high teacher once sent a note home to her mother stating, "You and your husband would be remiss in your duties if you do not see to it that this child goes to college."[2]

Only one of her family members had attended college, but Morrison was primed to excel in higher education as well. Her mother, Ramah Wofford, taught her to read when Morrison was still a preschooler. At three, she was already writing on sidewalks with her elder sister, Lois, and by the time she reached kindergarten, Morrison was the only literate child in her class. Ramah took part in a book club, and her love of literature rubbed off on both of her daughters. Morrison especially enjoyed books by British, Russian, French, and American authors, including Jane Austen, Leo Tolstoy, Fyodor Dostoevsky, Gustave Flaubert, and Mark Twain. She didn't yet know that she wanted to be a writer, but reading these authors influenced her to specifically write for African Americans, similarly to how the authors she admired wrote for readers who shared their ethnic backgrounds—be they Englishwomen or Eastern Europeans.

The literature she read brought joy to her childhood, but her early years weren't without challenges. While her father, George Wofford, worked as a welder, her mother was a homemaker, and the lack of a second income meant that money was often tight in the household. The Woffords bounced from residence to residence, and on one occasion when they couldn't cough up the rent money, their landlord set fire to their house, with them inside of it, according to Morrison, who was a small child at the time. The family chose to laugh at the landlord's "bizarre form of evil" instead of agonizing over his cruelty. This taught her to remain true to herself and her values in the wake of "monumental crudeness."[3]

Asked about her youth, she once said, "My parents made all of us feel as though there were these rather extraordinary deserving people within us. I felt like an aristocrat—or what I think an aristocrat is. I always knew we were very poor. But that was never degrading."[4]

When Morrison turned twelve, she helped her family financially by getting a job cleaning a wealthy white woman's home. She earned $2.50 weekly for her work, and she enjoyed seeing her wages go toward milk, insurance, and other household bills. But sometimes Morrison whined about her job, leading her father to warn her not to complain about work. "Listen. You don't live there," he said. "You live here. At home, with your people. Just go to work; get your money and come on home."[5] From this lesson, she learned not to overly identify with her job and to value her family life over her work life. Her role in her household and "village" took precedence over any role she performed for money.

Among Lorain's Black population, Morrison observed that people looked out for one another. She could count on African Americans from all walks of life to ensure that she and her sister were safe as they walked around town. In turn, she felt a sense of duty to her family and community as a youth. In addition to her job, Morrison had the responsibility of bringing walnuts to her grandfather and finding him when he wandered off. And just as *The Bluest Eye* notes how Aunt Jimmy's friend Miss Alice read the Bible to her, Morrison would read the Bible to her grandmother. In her community, no one lived for themselves alone. Everyone was interconnected, as her parents felt strongly that "all succor and aid came from themselves and their neighborhood."[6] She went on to pass along this same sense of village identity to her two sons to ensure that when they had their own children, "it won't be this little nuclear you and me, babe," she said.

Morrison's interactions with people outside the Black community could be complicated. Although her teachers and peers recognized that she was a promising young woman, the underlying racial tensions between Morrison and her white immigrant classmates sometimes bubbled to the surface. At first, these new arrivals to the country didn't exhibit racial prejudice, but the anti-Blackness of the United States would gradually change their perceptions of African Americans. Morrison said during a 1989 interview that if the United States did not have Black people, "the immigrants would've torn each other's throats out." Instead, this country taught them to find a common enemy in Black people. "Wherever they were from, they would stand together," she said of the nation's immigrants. "They could all say, 'I am not *that*.'"[7]

She recalled that a white immigrant boy sat next to her in the fifth grade. He was smart, but he didn't speak English, so she helped him with his reading. "I remember the moment he found out that I was Black—a nigger," she said. "It took him six months; he was told. And that's the moment when he belonged, that was his entrance."[8]

As a child, Morrison also observed the impact that her parents' Southern upbringings had on them. Her mother left Alabama at age six, but Ramah romanticized her native state as a wonderful place to live. Morrison figured that the truth was more complex, since Ramah never returned home. In contrast, Morrison's father made annual trips to his native Georgia, a place he supposedly hated. The couple's conflicting views of the South spilled over into their thoughts about white people too. When Morrison's father was about fourteen or fifteen, a white lynch mob killed two of his Black businessmen neighbors,[9] traumatizing him for life. She suspected that he saw the bodies of the men, and this gruesome incident led him to relocate to racially integrated Lorain, Ohio. He was far from the only African American who moved from the South to the North during this period. From 1916 to 1970, an estimated six million Black people left Southern towns for Northern cities as part of what historians now call the Great Migration. Like George Wofford, they fled segregation and racial violence and pursued better employment and educational opportunities for themselves and their children. But the racial terrorism George experienced in the South continued to color his interactions with white people after he settled in the Midwest.

"My father never trusted any white person at all, would not let them in his house, insurance people and so on," Morrison said. "Luckily my mother was entirely different, she was always judging people one at a time."[10]

When Morrison was a young girl, she watched her father throw a white man out of their apartment building for fear the stranger would harm her and her sister. In retrospect, Morrison believed he was mistaken; the man approaching their apartment was drunk but didn't have malicious intent. Nonetheless, knowing that her father was a protector and willing to have a physical confrontation with a white man on her behalf thrilled her. It taught her, she said, that it was possible for a Black person to win in this life.

Maternal Instincts

Unlike Pecola Breedlove's parents, Morrison's father accepted, protected, and cared for her. He never once even spanked her—and she viewed her mother as a hero as well. When Morrison was just an infant, her mother had to make a life-or-death decision on her behalf. A doctor told Ramah Wofford that her two small daughters had been exposed to tuberculosis (TB) and needed to be placed in a sanatorium. While Morrison was only a baby at the time, her big sister, Lois, born in 1929, was a toddler.

Ramah hesitated to place her young children in a tuberculosis hospital because the medical community still lacked best practices to treat TB in the 1930s. Also known as consumption or the "white plague," the disease is caused by a bacterium (*Mycobacterium tuberculosis*) that leads those unfortunate enough to breathe it in to experience hacking coughs, shortness of breath, extreme chest pain, and fatigue. In the 1800s, one in seven people infected with TB died from the condition, as scientists didn't identify the bacterium responsible until 1882.[11] By the 1920s, cases of tuberculosis in the United States waned due to public health campaigns about the importance of good hygiene, home visits by health inspectors, and "fresh air cures" that curbed the disease's spread. But when Morrison was born in 1931, the deadly condition was still quite common, and researchers had yet to find a remedy. It would take until 1943 before three biochemists—Selman Waksman, Albert Schatz, and Elizabeth Bugie—developed the antibiotic streptomycin to manage TB. And it would take until the 1950s before researchers coupled streptomycin with other drug therapies for a truly effective treatment of TB, since many patients relapsed when given streptomycin alone.

Aware that medical officials didn't know how to effectively manage TB, Ramah Wofford's intuition told her to ignore the doctor's advice to put her girls in a sanatorium. Health-care professionals primarily placed TB patients in such facilities to reduce the chances that these individuals would spread the disease to family members. In 1875, the country's first TB sanatorium opened in Asheville, North Carolina.[12] By 1904, 115 of these hospitals were in operation, and by 1953, a staggering 839 had launched. TB sanitariums may have been opening at a breakneck pace, but that didn't convince Ramah that her children would make it out of one alive.

"She simply saw that no one ever came out of those sanatoriums in the '30s, and also she had visitations" from ghosts, Morrison recalled in 1986. "It was interesting to me that they were treating tuberculosis patients at that time in a way that would kill them because they didn't have all of the right information."[13]

In fact, patients in TB sanatoriums died at roughly the same rate as individuals left untreated at home did. In either case, about half of the people afflicted with the disease succumbed to it. Ramah Wofford's sixth sense helped her make the shrewd decision to keep her children—who had only been exposed to tuberculosis, not formally diagnosed with it—out of the hospital and out of harm's way.

Morrison described the spiritual forces at work in her family members' lives as influences that went far beyond "a thing you do on Sunday morning in church."[14] She said spirituality informed their sensibilities in a way that she would not deem as magic but as reality. In her household, she recalled, adults discussed their dreams in the same way one might discuss "what really happened."[15] They also discussed visitations from ghosts and exhibited an intimate connection "with things that were not empirically verifiable."[16]

"It not only made them for me the most interesting people in the world—it was an enormous resource for the solution of certain kinds of problems," she said. "Without that, I think I would have been quite bereft because I would have been dependent on so-called scientific data to explain hopelessly unscientific things, and, also, I would have relied on information that even subsequent objectivity has proved to be fraudulent, you see."[17]

When Morrison said that she would rather write fiction because her own life didn't interest her, she overlooked how much she appreciated growing up with relatives who didn't distinguish between the dream world and the waking world, openly discussed paranormal experiences, and used their intuition to make both urgent and everyday decisions. Her grandmother, for example, would interpret dreams to play the numbers. Her family also believed that certain events in dreams represented events in real life—but often in an inverted way. A dream about a joyous occasion like a wedding signified that a somber occasion like a funeral was imminent.

Magical Realism

Morrison might have preferred fiction writing to memoir writing, but her early life directly influenced the topics she broached in her literature. Had Ramah Wofford not practiced the African American oral tradition, telling her daughter endless stories, it's doubtful that Morrison would've become a writer. Ramah didn't just have visitations from spirits but frequently told Morrison ghost stories passed down from her own mother and aunt. In 1982, Ramah told the *Lorain Journal* how Morrison would beg, "Mama, please tell the story about this or that. Finally, I'd get tired of telling the stories over and over again. So, I made up a new story."[18]

Morrison learned to emulate her mother, spending her free time telling stories and visiting the public library with her sister, Lois, whom she was closer to than her younger brothers. Like the sisters Claudia and Frieda MacTeer of *The Bluest Eye*, she and Lois were constantly together, so much so that friends would refer to them as a unit— "Loisandchloe! Loisandchloe!"—instead of as individuals.[19] To her family members, she was always Chloe, even after she became famous as Toni Morrison.

The close relationship that the MacTeer sisters have isn't the only part of *The Bluest Eye* inspired by Morrison's life. The book takes place in Lorain, Ohio, and it contains the storytelling traditions that Morrison grew up with as a girl. The narrator describes how a young Cholly Breedlove gets a job at a feed and grain store where he meets an elderly man and storyteller nicknamed Blue Jack: "Blue used to tell him old-timey stories about how it was when the Emancipation Proclamation came. How the black people hollered, cried, and sang. And ghost stories about how a white man cut off his wife's head and buried her in the swamp, and the headless body came out at night and went stumbling around the yard, knocking over stuff because it couldn't see, and crying all the time for a comb."[20]

The Bluest Eye characters recite ghost stories and know their Bible well, with Aunt Jimmy telling Cholly she didn't name him Samson Fuller after his birth father because "ain't no Samson never come to no good end."[21] The biblical Samson, of course, died after his lover, Delilah, arranged for a servant to cut his long hair, a breach of the Nazirite vow that gave him superhuman strength. After Aunt Jimmy's own demise, it's clear that signs and premonitions play significant roles in the lives of her friends. They say they should have known she was about to die when she asked for black thread, a symbol of death. These women, along with characters such as Blue Jack, M'Dear, and the MacTeer sisters, don't believe in a strictly rational world because African Americans historically have not. More specifically, they represent Morrison's family members who were as familiar with Scripture as they were with dream interpretation.

"Black people believe in magic," Morrison told the *New York Times* in 1977. "Once a woman asked me, Do you believe in ghosts? I said, 'Yes. Do you believe in germs?' It's part of our heritage."[22]

As early as the novel's third page, the word *magic* appears, and it is repeated in a subsequent passage about the strange hold little white girls have on adults—both Black and white. To Morrison, *magic* was not synonymous with the term *make-believe,* and she objected when critics described her books as magical realism because she regarded that label as an evasive one used to cover up a literary work's deeper meaning. "If you could apply the word 'magical,'" she argued, "then that dilutes the realism, but it seemed legitimate because there were these supernatural and unrealistic things, surreal things, going on in the text."[23] Magical realism, she said, gave critics a convenient way to ignore the "truth in the art of certain writers," usually ones who weren't white Americans.[24]

The term *magic realism* dates back to the 1920s German art world, when critic Franz Roh used the expression *magischer Realismus* to describe a style of painting called

Neue Sachlichkeit, or New Objectivity, which focused on the magical nature of the "real" world.[25] Shortly afterward, the Italian writer Massimo Bontempelli applied the term to writing, starting a magic realist magazine in 1926. The movement went on to influence the work of Latin American writers, including literary critic Angel Flores, who wrote the 1955 essay "Magical Realism in Spanish American Fiction." The piece stands out for reportedly using the term *magical realism*, rather than *magic realism*, for the first time.

In the decades that followed, critics labeled fiction that portrayed magical events as ordinary occurrences in the lives of characters as magical realism. This literary genre differs from fantasy in that the world portrayed is not removed from reality; it simply has magical components that tend to make compelling statements about reality. Today, magical realism is mostly linked to the literature of Latin American writers such as Gabriel García Márquez and Isabel Allende, another reason the term does not quite fit Morrison's work, which is steeped in African American culture.

"My own use of enchantment simply comes because that's the way the world was for me and for the Black people I knew," she said during a 1986 interview. "In addition to the very shrewd, down-to-earth, efficient way in which they did things and survived things, there was this other knowledge or perception, always discredited but nevertheless there, which informed their sensibilities and clarified their activities. It formed a kind of cosmology that was perceptive as well as enchanting, and so it seemed impossible for me to write about Black people and eliminate that simply because it was 'unbelievable.'"[26]

In Morrison's fiction, the use of magic is not a literary device but her way of highlighting the enduring belief systems of Black Americans. While this demographic may be overwhelmingly Christian, slavery did not completely sever their ties with West African spiritual practices, such as visiting healers when ill, consulting diviners, owning sacred objects, or maintaining relationships with their ancestors. In fact, West African spirituality played key roles in Denmark Vesey's foiled 1822 slave rebellion in South Carolina and in the Haitian Revolution, which took place from 1791 to 1804.

Jacob K. Olupona, a professor of African religious traditions at Harvard Divinity School, has described indigenous African spirituality as "an oral tradition that has never been fully codified." It recognizes, he said, "that beliefs and practices touch on and inform every facet of human life, and therefore African religion cannot be separated from the everyday or mundane."[27]

Olupona's remarks about indigenous African religion echo Morrison's recollections about the African Americans in her life experiencing supernatural phenomena but going about their days unfazed. His comments also explain why the term *magical realism* doesn't fully capture Morrison's work. Although she used the word *magic* in her books, she was really describing the West African beliefs that Europeans trivialized as "magic," "witchcraft," and "superstition." Morrison acknowledged as much, pointing out to an interviewer that these traditions aren't new or even unique to Black people: "It's just that, when it comes from discredited people, it somehow has some other exotic attachment: Thus, the word 'magic.'"[28]

As an author who crafted "indisputably Black" fiction, Morrison presented African American folklore, religion, and supernatural elements in her novels to pass on these traditions to her readers. She lamented that Black people are no longer as familiar with African American mythology because they have moved away from small towns and into cities without the same cultural ties and storytelling customs. She included herself in that category, pointing out that she left Lorain to pursue higher education and a career in academia and publishing. "It was a sacrifice," she said. "There is a certain sense of family I don't have. So, the myths get forgotten."[29]

The actor Michael B. Jordan is a case in point. He sparked a backlash after telling *Vanity Fair* in October 2018 that "we don't have any mythology, Black mythology, or folklore. Creating our own mythology is very important because it helps [people] dream."[30] African Americans promptly took to Twitter to correct the *Black Panther* star, and a month later, he clarified his comments. He argued that Black mythologies and folklore aren't presented in film and television and that he wanted to use these media to pass along the stories he heard as a child. Rather than film, Morrison believed that the novel was one of the best ways to pass on the "classical mythological archetypal stories" that Black parents once told their children.[31] For contemporary African Americans, she asserted, the novel has never been more important because it serves an important role in transmitting this information.

The transition of African Americans out of small towns and into big cities wasn't the only reason growing numbers of this population no longer understood the folklore and spirituality of their ancestors. Morrison acknowledged that some young people simply weren't interested in this way of life. "They don't want to hark back to those embarrassing days when we were associated with 'haints' [restless spirits] and superstitions," she said.[32]

But Morrison was shortsighted to hold young people entirely responsible for this trend, as doing so ignores the historic criminalization of traditional African-based spirituality in the United States and throughout the Americas. Additionally, this argument ignores shifts in American popular culture, which was fixated on the customs and beliefs of the foreign "other" when Morrison was born in 1931. The nation's interest in the exotic would wane as the decades passed.

Exotifying and Demonizing African American Culture

In 1935, four years after Toni Morrison's birth, the writer and anthropologist Zora Neale Hurston's book *Mules and Men* debuted. The collection includes folklore and folk traditions that Hurston, who would go on to write the groundbreaking 1937 novel *Their Eyes Were Watching God*, compiled during trips to her hometown of Eatonville, Florida, as well as to Polk County, Florida, and New Orleans. Hurston received praise for documenting more than seventy folktales that might not have been recorded in written form without her efforts. The same year that *Mules and Men* came out, the folklorist and Anglican minister Harry Middleton Hyatt's book *Folk-Lore from Adams County Illinois* was published. Unlike *Mules and Men*, Hyatt's book takes place in the Midwest and includes the folklore and traditions of people from various ethnic groups, including Irish Americans, German Americans, and African Americans. He would later travel to the South to record folk customs specific to Black people; the results of this undertaking appear in his 1970 collection *Hoodoo—Conjuration—Witchcraft—Rootwork*.

Today, both Hyatt and Hurston stand out for their endeavors to preserve US folk customs when such undertakings weren't common practice, but as a Black woman doing this work, Hurston had a personal connection to her African American subjects that Hyatt did not. In line with the time period's respectability politics—the idea that adopting white middle-class standards of dress, behavior, and morality will protect marginalized groups from harm—many Black writers focused on affluent African American professionals in their works. In contrast, Hurston concentrated on Black storytellers from rural and impoverished backgrounds in *Mules and Men*. These African Americans were in many ways the cultural innovators of the Black community, having pioneered art forms such as jazz and blues and preserved the Black oral tradition.

Because it highlights Black people who didn't belong to the "Talented Tenth," the term sociologist W. E. B. DuBois popularized in 1903 to refer to the elite and educated classes of African Americans, *Mules and Men* doesn't appear to cater to the white gaze. But the truth is much thornier. Hurston wrote and conducted research for the book with the help of a wealthy white benefactor named Charlotte Osgood

Mason, who has since been accused of trying to control the works of the Black artists she supported. Specifically, scholars have criticized the socialite for her overwhelming interest in depictions of "primitive" African Americans and for depriving the Black creators she sponsored of the opportunity to own their work. "It is difficult to believe that Hurston was blind to the cultural imperialism, the white supremacy of her sponsor, Mrs. Mason," the feminist and scholar bell hooks argues in *Yearning: Race, Gender, and Cultural Politics*.[33] Ultimately, hooks concluded that Hurston must have determined that sharing Black culture with the broader public was the most effective way to prevent African American folk traditions from disappearing, much like Morrison thought the novel could be used to pass down Black folklore and mythology to younger generations of Black people.

The "cultural imperialism" that hooks attributes to Charlotte Osgood Mason wasn't unique to the socialite. During the years immediately before and after Morrison's birth, white America took a particular interest in cultures it deemed exotic—be they from Egypt, the Orient, South Asia, Harlem, or the African American South. The 1922 discovery of King Tut's tomb heightened the Western fascination with the foreign "other," a fixation reflected in the architecture and interior design of theaters, Hollywood films, fashion trends, and advertisements. Hollywood Golden Age actresses such as Lana Turner, Joan Crawford, and Marlene Dietrich routinely wore turbans, and perfume and makeup ads featured sketches of women in feathered head wraps holding crystal balls as wafts of incense smoke enshrouded them. The products advertised promised to return a lost love or prevent him from straying, and many targeted African Americans, a clientele that had been just as exotified as the "foreigners" in the ads.

In the early twentieth century, Black Americans still contended with racist stereotypes that framed them as a primitive people because of their roots in Africa and, by extension, the jungle—despite the fact that jungles, or rainforests, make up a small portion of the continent. White Americans and Europeans viewed Black music, dance, and religion through the exotic lens of the other, and some African Americans internalized or capitalized on these stereotypes. The African American dancer Josephine Baker, for example, rose to fame in 1920s Paris performing the Danse Sauvage with exposed breasts, a skirt made of mock bananas, and a pet cheetah. An immensely talented singer, dancer, and actor, Baker's popularity grew by presenting Black womanhood as hypersexual and "savage" for European audiences who subscribed to such stereotypes.

Critic Pierre de Régnier, who reviewed her show at the time, even used animalistic terms to describe Baker's performance of the Danse Sauvage. "She is in constant motion, her body writhing like a snake or more precisely like a dipping saxophone," he said. "Music seems to pour from her body. She grimaces, crosses her eyes, wiggles disjointedly, does a split and finally crawls off the stage stiff-legged, her rump higher than her head, like a young giraffe."[34]

While Baker leaned into the primitive stereotype— some argue that she subverted it by controlling her own narrative—African Americans bound by respectability politics resisted this characterization of their people. They were eager to demonstrate that Black Americans were rational, dignified, and morally decent. The Harlem Renaissance writer Nella Larsen described this tendency in her 1928 novella *Quicksand*, in which protagonist Helga Crane, loosely based on the author, reminds herself that she isn't a "jungle creature" after a visit to a Harlem nightclub with a "wild, murky orchestra" that resulted in the patrons "shaking themselves ecstatically to a thumping of unseen tom-toms."[35] Helga is a former teacher at a Black college where officials are so concerned that their young charges will fall prey to their primal instincts that students are discouraged from wearing bright colors such as yellow, green, or red. Instead, everyone must wear black, gray, navy blue, or brown, lest their latent savagery emerge.

Aware of how white people stereotyped African Americans as primitive, Larsen takes her novella from the nightclubs of Harlem to a preacher's home in the Deep South. Her biracial protagonist, raised by white family members until they abandon her, assumes that marrying a Black pastor who lives in a rural community will give her an authentic African American experience, but the relationship is a trap. As a Black pastor's wife, she is bound by gender and cultural norms that result in her having a succession of children and little else, a fate that drains her physically, mentally, and spiritually. *Quicksand* illustrates how village life can be confining for Black women—a point that Morrison's *Sula* also makes—and rejects the idea that a down-home rural lifestyle is the only genuine one for African Americans. The book also explores how the idea that

African Americans are inherently uncivilized harms the psyche and inhibits them from expressing their full humanity. That Larsen tacitly made this argument in her work during a time when wealthy white voyeurs demanded an insider's view of the Black experience—and authenticity to them meant either "simple" Southern folk or "wild" Harlem clubgoers—distinguishes her from the African American artists willing to lean into this stereotype.

The white socialite Charlotte Osgood Mason bankrolled not just Zora Neale Hurston's career but the careers of Harlem Renaissance legends Langston Hughes, Alain Locke, Aaron Douglas, and Miguel Covarrubias as well. While this powerful New Yorker wanted to know the ins and outs of African American artistic, folkloric, and hoodoo traditions, other whites viewed Black folk practices as threatening, irrational, or both. Particularly, the customs related to indigenous African spirituality were criminalized, which drove them underground.

With origins in African traditional religious cultures, hoodoo is a form of spirituality in which practitioners known as root workers or conjurers perform rituals, apply herbal and plant-based remedies, honor God and their ancestors, and use sacred objects. When *The Bluest Eye*'s M'Dear treats an ailing Aunt Jimmy, she engages in some of these practices. Her hickory stick is a sacred object that she uses to perform the ritual of discovering the source of Jimmy's sickness. M'Dear also instructs Jimmy's caregivers to complete their own ritual—burying their patient's "slop jar and everything in it." And M'Dear's remedy is plant based, as she tells Jimmy to drink pot liquor, or the liquid residue of cooked greens, for two days straight and nothing else. Before Jimmy falls ill, the reader learns that she engages in the hoodoo practice of wearing the asafetida bag—a sacred object and herbal remedy in one. Morrison does not use the term *hoodoo* to describe these practices, but they easily fall into this folk tradition, also known as rootwork or conjure and commonly described as folk magic. Just as Morrison raised concern about white people labeling African American spirituality "magic" instead of part of reality, so have some hoodoo experts.

In her 2020 book *The Hoodoo Tarot*, author Tayannah Lee McQuillar apologized for previously describing hoodoo as magic. She explained that she did so "in an attempt to assimilate the topic to academic language and standards." She went on to say, "Hoodoo wasn't folk magic when it started being described as such by social scientists, nor is it folk magic now. . . . It is the product of people who faced terrorism and unimaginable suffering on a daily basis yet refused to relinquish all of their power and identity. Hoodoo, in addition to being a body of botanical and esoteric knowledge, is also a rebellion against absolute mental and spiritual domination by Europeans."[36]

Whites have historically suppressed, vilified, and criminalized hoodoo as deviancy or quackery even though many of the African Americans who traditionally practiced hoodoo identified as Christians. In fact, these practitioners would often recite passages from the book of Psalms and other parts of the Bible as they took part in hoodoo customs. Debates about the "validity" of African-based folk and religious traditions took place as early as the antebellum period, with Southern states such as Tennessee in 1831 prohibiting African American root workers from practicing folk medicine. According to anthropologist Tony Kail's 2017 book *A Secret History of Memphis Hoodoo*, evidence of the smear campaign against hoodoo can be found in newspaper headlines as far back as the 1860s.

Nashville's *Daily Union and American* newspaper portrayed hoodoo as a sinister tradition and accused practitioners of grave digging and conducting human sacrifices. "It may not be generally known to the public," the paper stated in 1866, "but it is nevertheless a fact, that these barbarous African superstitions and practices are increasing among the freedman of Memphis and Tennessee but of all the Southern states."[37] Moreover, the *Memphis Public Ledger* framed hoodoo practitioners as threats to white Americans, and in turn, these individuals became the targets of racial violence and aggressive and biased policing. In 1869, officers conducted a raid in an African American neighborhood of Memphis during which they confiscated root workers' herbs and ritual tools. The vilification of conjurers as con artists, killers, and drug traffickers certainly didn't help their reputation.[38]

To be sure, some people, both Black and white, did pretend to have spiritual gifts to take people's hard-earned money. This phenomenon wasn't lost on Morrison, who includes such a character, Soaphead Church, in *The Bluest Eye*. This unscrupulous man, a self-described "reader, adviser, and interpreter of dreams," convinces Pecola Breedlove that God will answer her prayer for blue eyes if she performs a "ritual" that, unbeknownst to her, will lead to a dog's death.[39]

Although hoodoo sometimes attracted con artists, the tradition itself derives from genuine indigenous West African principles and produced many skilled practitioners like M'Dear. When the press and the police weren't slandering this tradition, they were ridiculing it as primitive and foolish. Concurrently, white-owned companies such as Keystone Laboratories, Lucky Heart Cosmetics, and Collins Laboratories moved to the Memphis area, where they sold herbs, oils, powders, and sachets geared toward root workers and conjurers. As influential white-run institutions made a point to demean indigenous African religious cultures, white entrepreneurs profited from these traditions.

As late as the 1960s, the legal system continued to create barriers for African American folk practitioners. Police raids of root workers went on, and municipalities prohibited spiritual readers from doing their work without a license. Those who violated the law could be charged with a misdemeanor, a fine, and jail time. The government had effectively criminalized and regulated traditional African religion, requiring a $750 fee to operate in some cities.[40] Given this, African Americans did not simply move away from small towns and lose interest in their folk practices, as Morrison suggested. They adapted after the state systematically forced them to distance themselves from their ancestral customs, all the while denigrating these traditions as silly and evil.

In her fiction, Morrison uplifted the discredited practices her family members exposed her to throughout her childhood. By crafting characters who discuss their dreams, have ghostly visitations, and foretell the future in the same vein that the elders she knew purportedly did, Morrison illustrated how African-based spirituality enriches the lives of Black Americans. Such a cosmology did not constitute magical realism to the people in her community or to their counterparts in her novels. Instead, this worldview informed everything from the day-to-day decisions they made to their major life choices, making it very practical knowledge.

While Morrison valued African American spiritual customs, as a youth, she also felt drawn to the church, particularly the Catholic Church. This set her apart from her parents but drew her closer to her Catholic extended family members who piqued her interest in this religion rife with rituals unrecognized by her mother's AME denomination. For centuries, Catholicism's network of saints and reverence for the Virgin Mary has made it attractive to diasporic Africans accustomed to spiritual systems that include the veneration of women and ancestors alike.

3

Black and Catholic

A Long Tradition

"Who refers to Toni Morrison as a Catholic novelist?"[1]

Critic Patrick Giles poses this question in his *Los Angeles Times* book review of *The Life You Save May Be Your Own* (2003), which examines how Catholicism influenced the lives and literature of four writers: Flannery O'Connor, Dorothy Day, Thomas Merton, and Walker Percy.

"Religion remains a source of disquiet in American literary culture," Giles argued. "Even though many of our greatest stories and poems ripple with faith-based tribulations as powerful as the sea swallowing the Pequod, critics and readers shy away from discussing the frankly religious temper of so many of our writers."[2]

Having named her books *Song of Solomon, Beloved, Paradise* (1997), *Love* (2003), *A Mercy* (2008), and *God Help the*

Child (2015), Morrison left no doubt that her work explores religious themes. The titles alone make it obvious to people who've never cracked open one of her novels. Yet critics typically focus on the ways that being a Black woman informed Morrison's writing and ignore the role that Catholicism played in her life and literature. Giles might have pondered why Morrison isn't widely described as a Catholic novelist, but even he failed to explain why they should. He devotes a single line in his piece—a question in parentheses—to Morrison's faith background.

Catholicism, however, did not exist in the margins of Morrison's life. As a child, she made a deliberate decision to join the Catholic Church, a religious institution that didn't have a large African American membership in the 1940s, when she became a member. During the intervening years, Morrison remained devoted to the faith, raising her two sons Catholic when she became a mother and drawing on Catholicism in her literature when she became a literary star in middle age.

To frame Black women as divine in her fiction, Morrison employs both the persecution of Jesus Christ and the suffering of Mary, underscoring her Catholic identity. Catholics revere and highlight the Blessed Virgin in their faith in a way that's largely unfamiliar to Protestants, who recognize her as Christ's mother but don't venerate or fixate on her. In Morrison's fiction, however, this religious icon routinely appears. She can be found in paintings in characters' homes, in the powerful women characters capable of working miracles, or in the Black mother characters grieving for their children as she grieved for Jesus. Using Mary to emphasize the strength and suffering of Black women suggests that while Morrison broadly engaged womanist theology in her works, she specifically engaged a Catholic womanist theology.

The focus on corporeality in her literature also distinguishes Morrison as a Catholic novelist, and in none of her books is the focus on the body greater than it is in *Beloved*, writer Nicholas Ripatrazone told me during a 2017 interview. He argues, *"Beloved* is her most Catholic book, because it is almost exclusively a theology of the body—how [the protagonist] Sethe's body is burned, scarred, and a place of sacrilege; how [her daughter] Beloved's body is both flesh and spirit, how a home and a place and a memory can each be forms of bodies. This strikes me as profoundly Catholic, and not at all Protestant. When I think of Protestants, I think of the cross; when I think of Catholics, I think of the crucifix."[3]

With nuns, an ersatz convent, and Afro-Catholic spirituality playing a central role in the story line, Morrison's *Paradise* also stands out as one of her most Catholic novels. But Morrison, Ripatrazone noted, has often been mistaken for a Protestant. That's in large part because she did not discuss her faith at length, and interviewers usually did not ask her to elaborate on the significance of Catholicism in her life. The fact that Morrison never detailed the ins and outs of her relationship with the church does not signal a detachment from religion. On the contrary, it indicates that she viewed it as a deeply intimate matter worth protecting from public scrutiny, just as she protected her children and her personal life generally from such scrutiny. Likening her to F. Scott Fitzgerald, the *New York Times* described Morrison as "intensely private," and her faith mostly fell behind the curtain that she declared off-limits to the public.

Discussing her novel *Paradise*, in which she engages religion explicitly rather than implicitly, Morrison revealed that she viewed faith as a sacred matter that deserved her respect. She said, "I am a Catholic; some of my family is Catholic, some of them are Protestant, some of them are all sorts of things. And what saved me was, I think—what helped me at any rate [in writing this book]—was knowing that I was going to take religion seriously. . . . It wasn't going to be ironic. I wasn't going to be—these are people who see things, who envision things, who act on things that come, and I wasn't going to disparage it, and I wasn't going to comment on it."[4]

Morrison's decision to be reticent about religion, be it in relation to her books or her life, explains why there's so little information about what Catholicism meant to her specifically. She told the public what she thought they should know: she was a Catholic, she took matters of faith seriously, and that wasn't up for debate.

Anthony of Padua: Morrison's Namesake

As a child, Catholic rituals fascinated Morrison. Through the Catholic wing of her family, she likely saw her young relatives preparing for their First Communion, the rite of passage marking an individual's initial Eucharist. In this ceremony, Christians eat and drink bread and wine in honor of the bread and wine Jesus Christ and his apostles feasted on during the Last Supper, his final meal before the crucifixion. For the occasion, the communicants wear formal clothing. While boys usually wear suits and ties, girls wear veils and white dresses, similar to the burial clothes *The Bluest Eye*'s Aunt Jimmy wore. Afterward, families usually celebrate by throwing a party.

"Low church" Protestant sects, such as the AME denomination to which Morrison's mother belonged, don't mark First Communion with elaborate ceremonies, so as a child drawn to ritual, Morrison must have felt deprived seeing young family members experience a rite of passage her church did not observe. Ultimately, her interest in rituals and her relationship with a devout Catholic relative would drive her to convert as a twelve-year-old. Of her Catholic family members, Morrison told NPR in 2015, "One . . . was a cousin with whom I was very close, and she was a Catholic. And, so, I got baptized, et cetera, and I chose Saint Anthony of Padua as the baptismal name."[5] This baptismal name is exactly why Morrison became famous as "Toni" rather than as Chloe, her birth name.

Now a popular name for American girls, Chloe was a relatively rare name during Morrison's formative years, she said. Outside her family, few people properly pronounced the name, which is of Greek origin and another moniker for Demeter, the goddess of the harvest and fertility. It also appears in the Bible when the Apostle Paul in First Corinthians 1:11 says in a letter to the Corinthians that "some from Chloe's household have informed me that there are quarrels among you." It is fitting that a woman so interested in mythology, the church, and the divine feminine had a given name steeped in all these frameworks. Morrison would go on to name a character First Corinthians, after the book of the Bible containing the sole scriptural reference to "Chloe."

Morrison publicly left her birth name behind when she moved away from Lorain to attend Howard University in Washington, DC, and someone mistakenly called her "Toni." She decided to stick with the new moniker because people could pronounce it correctly, and Toni happened to be a shortened version of her baptismal name. To her family, though, she would always remain Chloe; Lois Wofford even named one of her children Chloe after her younger sister.

Just as Morrison's given name suited her on multiple levels, so did her chosen baptismal name. Her first novel wasn't published until she was thirty-nine, but when she was baptized in the Catholic Church at twelve, Morrison had the foresight to name herself after a saint who had both a way with words and a connection to Africa.

Born Fernando Martins de Bulhões into a noble Portuguese family in 1195, Anthony of Padua stood out during his short life (he died at thirty-five) for his excellent knowledge of Scripture, masterful sermons, and outreach to the sick and the poor. According to legend, he's responsible for the "miracle of the fish," which reportedly occurred after he visited the Italian city of Rimini, known at the time for its large population of heretics.[6] The leaders and people of the town ignored him, causing Anthony to pray and meditate in response. He took a walk afterward and happened upon the Marecchia River, where he delivered a spontaneous sermon to the fish in this body of water, the mouth of which streams into the Adriatic Sea.

"You, fish of the river and sea, listen to the Word of God because the heretics do not wish to hear it," Anthony told them.[7] In an instant, according to the lore about this saint, rows of fish appeared, their heads just above the water as if they understood his message. When the townspeople saw this miraculous sight, they decided to hear what Anthony had to say, ultimately finding his words so touching that they reconsidered the church after years of heresy.

In addition to his preaching—unique for its use of symbols and allegory to analyze Scripture—Anthony is known as the patron saint of lost or stolen things. Legend has it that during his time in Bologna, Italy, Anthony, who was a teacher as well as a preacher, lost a psalm book that included his instructional notes for his students.[8] He prayed to be reunited with the psalter, as the printing press would not be invented until the fifteenth century, and any books created prior to this innovation were copied by hand and expensive to make. Having taken a vow of poverty, he would not have been able to easily obtain another such book, but the Franciscan novice who took it felt inspired to give it back after Anthony's heartfelt prayers.

During a 2017 *Granta* magazine interview, writer Mario Kaiser asked Morrison which lost things she'd like to have again, given her namesake saint. "Two things," she answered. "One is my son. And there are certain periods in my life I'd like to live over."[9] Tragically, Morrison's son Slade Morrison died from complications of pancreatic cancer in 2010. As for the periods of her life that she wanted to experience again, she named her college years but specifically focused on a time that church members cared for her. She recalled that while traveling with her college theater troupe in the segregated South, the group's accommodation plans fell through, so the faculty member overseeing the trip contacted a Black preacher to see if any of his congregants would house them. Within fifteen minutes, the pastor found church members willing to put up the students.

"I went with a girl, stayed in this woman's house," Morrison remembered. "It was fabulous! God, she had dried her sheets on bushes that had that odor. Oh, it was heaven! And they fixed us fabulous food. We tried to give them money, but they wouldn't take it. So, we put it in the pillowslip."[10]

Her favorite college memory didn't concern parties, boys, friendships, or a fascinating lecture she once heard; it was about the church—particularly Black Christians and their generosity to her and her fellow students who would've been stranded in the Jim Crow South without their help. This was the time in her life that she wanted to revisit, which reveals how much she valued both the African American community and Christian charity.

Having grown up in African American Protestant churches before her Catholic conversion, it's unclear how much Morrison knew about Anthony of Padua, also known as Anthony of Lisbon, when she was baptized with the name or how much she knew about him as an adult because she said next to nothing about the saint publicly. Anthony had some distinct ties to Africa, since his namesake was Anthony the Great, an Egyptian monk celebrated for spreading the concept of monasticism among Christians. For his efforts,

Anthony the Great is known as the "father of all monks." And Anthony of Padua named himself after this legendary monk when he encountered a hermitage for Franciscan friars shortly after his ordination to the priesthood. Because the hermitage bore the monk's name and Anthony appreciated the Franciscans' simple way of life, he began to use it as his own. Later, when word spread that five Franciscan friars had been martyred in Morocco, Anthony, unafraid for his own safety, traveled to North Africa to be of service.

Anthony wasn't ignorant of oppression and its impact, noting that it could be spiritual, emotional, physical, economic, or political in nature.[11] He believed that Christians had the responsibility of releasing both themselves and others from the bonds of oppression, an opinion Morrison shared. "Your real job is that if you are free, you need to free somebody else," she said. "If you have some power, then your job is to empower somebody else."[12]

Black Catholics in the United States

The idea that people who have unchained themselves from oppression also have a duty to free others aligns with both the Black and Catholic liberation theologies. In the US Catholic Church, however, African Americans didn't find a refuge from racism. They had to wage a battle against bigotry within that institution just as the founders of the AME Church did in their own religious order. Although Black Catholics have been a presence in the Americas since the 1500s, the Black Catholic movement for equality didn't begin until the twentieth century, when large numbers of

African Americans converted to Catholicism, all the while facing racial prejudice from white church members.

During the Great Migration of African Americans from the rural South to the industrialized North, millions of Black people moved into cities with large Catholic populations. Among them were Morrison's family members, a branch of whom became Catholic, likely after settling in Midwestern communities with an influx of European Catholic immigrants. In 1900, for instance, only a few hundred Black Catholics called Chicago home, but by 1975, the number had grown to eighty thousand.[13] The nationwide population of African American Catholics also grew exponentially—from about three hundred thousand in 1940 to roughly a million in 1975. Today, the United States is home to an estimated three million Black Catholics, a larger membership than that of the AME Church and 4 percent of the US Catholic Church membership overall.[14]

As Black Catholics grew in number, they often encountered racism from white Catholics who tried to stop them from becoming homeowners in their communities or took part in white flight, leaving behind racially diverse cities and parishes for mostly white suburbs. That many of these Catholics came from immigrant backgrounds and faced xenophobia in the United States didn't matter. As Morrison said while reflecting on her white immigrant classmate from the fifth grade, "Becoming an American is based on an attitude: an exclusion of me. It wasn't negative to them—it was unifying. When they got off the boat, the second word they learned was 'nigger.'"[15]

The Catholic clergy leaves behind a more complex legacy. While they weren't necessarily antiracist, a number of priests and nuns proselytized to the African Americans in their neighborhoods and encouraged the parents in particular to place their children in parochial schools. This exposed African Americans to Catholic traditions, inspiring tens of thousands to join the church. Had the clergy ignored these potential converts on the basis of race, like the whites who left racially diverse parishes did, it's doubtful that Black people would have joined the church in detectable numbers. Nuns and priests wanted African Americans to repent and be saved—their same goal for any other group of people—but that didn't mean they treated their charges as equals behind church doors. The Catholic Church has been implicated in the enslavement of African Americans and in the enforcement of racial segregation.

The social unrest in the United States during the civil rights and Black Power movements led African American Catholics to call out the church for perpetuating racism. After the Reverend Martin Luther King Jr.'s 1968 assassination, the Black Catholic Clergy Caucus, the National Black Sisters' Conference, and the National Convention of Black Lay Catholics challenged themselves and the church to fight for the liberation and empowerment of African Americans and acknowledge the immorality of racial oppression. Some Black Catholic activists also argued that Black parishes needed Black clergy members to lead them, while others joined forces with the Chicago Black Panther Party.

In light of the concerns Black Catholics raised and the racial uprisings sweeping the country, the US Catholic bishops in 1970 approved the National Office for Black Catholics in Washington, DC. Fourteen years later, "the 10 Black bishops of the United States declared that the Black Catholic community in the United States had 'come of age,'" according to Matthew J. Cressler, author of *Authentically Black and Truly Catholic: The Rise of Black Catholicism in the Great Migration*. "After more than a decade of activism, scholarship, and struggle, it was finally possible for black Catholics to be, in their words, both 'authentically Black' and 'truly Catholic.'"[16]

During the tumultuous years leading up to the approval of the National Office for Black Catholics, Morrison had not been marching in the streets or engaging in other kinds of political protest. She did not raise the church's history of race relations as a concern about Catholicism. Rather, she objected to some of the changes that stemmed from the Second Vatican Council, which called more than two thousand church leaders, officials, and laypeople together for four sessions at St. Peter's Basilica between 1962 and 1965 to review and develop church practices and doctrine in the contemporary world. Morrison recalled the ambivalence she felt about Catholicism after Vatican II during an interview for Antonio Monda's 2007 book *Do You Believe? Conversations on God and Religion*. "I had a moment of crisis on the occasion of Vatican II," she said. "At the time I had the impression that it was a superficial change, and I suffered greatly from the abolition of Latin, which I saw as the unifying and universal language of the Church."[17]

But she also appreciated some of the changes Vatican II introduced: "I still find the revolution of love that replaced the idea of justice astonishing," she told Monto. "It's something extremely modern, and perhaps eternal, which someone brought to humanity."[18]

A loving nature is the characteristic that unites the holiest women in Morrison's works, including *Song of Solomon*'s Pilate Dead, *Beloved*'s Baby Suggs, and *Paradise*'s Consolata Sosa. The love of these women nourishes, transforms, and empowers the hurting people in their lives, which points to their godliness. While love is central to the Christian faith, many believers, including Morrison, have found themselves at times yearning for justice.

The rise of the Black Lives Matter movement and the 2016 election of Donald Trump as president, which coincided with a spike in hate crimes, renewed conversations about the role of racial equality in the Catholic Church. More than half (60 percent) of white Catholics voted for Trump then, despite his campaign promise to build a wall along the US-Mexico border and decision to stereotype Mexican migrants as rapists and criminals.[19] In 1989, Trump called for the execution of the Central Park Five, a group of Black teens who were later vindicated of the crime of raping a white woman jogger in the iconic New York City park. And he and his late father faced a federal lawsuit in 1973 for allegedly discriminating against African American renters in their apartment buildings. That the charges of racism against Trump didn't deter white Catholics from voting for him drew attention to the racial divisions in the church once more.

After Trump won the 2016 presidential race, Morrison penned a *New Yorker* essay called "Making America White

Again," a play on his campaign slogan, "Make America Great Again." Expressing the views of many African Americans, Catholic or otherwise, Morrison stated,

> On Election Day, how eagerly so many white voters—both the poorly educated and the well educated—embraced the shame and fear sowed by Donald Trump. The candidate whose company has been sued by the Justice Department for not renting apartments to Black people. The candidate who questioned whether Barack Obama was born in the United States, and who seemed to condone the beating of a Black Lives Matter protester at a campaign rally. The candidate who kept Black workers off the floors of his casinos. The candidate who is beloved by David Duke and endorsed by the Ku Klux Klan.[20]

Morrison's use of repetition to condemn "the candidate" is a hallmark of the Black oral tradition, in which words and phrases are repeated to allow listeners to actively engage in the language of storytellers—be they griots or preachers. Even in an essay about white racism, printed in an elite non-Black publication like the *New Yorker*, Morrison still chose to write in a style familiar to any African American churchgoer. She specifically invoked such Christians in her essay when she described how white supremacy has historically and recently endangered Black congregants. She recalled the 1963 killing of four Black girls in a racially motivated Alabama church bombing, the 2015 fatal shooting of nine African Americans by a white supremacist at a South Carolina church, and the periodic burnings of Black churches that have taken place for decades. Morrison also appealed to the oppressor's sense of morality in her piece, arguing that white supremacists "have begun to do things they clearly don't really want to be doing, and, to do so, they are (1) abandoning their sense of human dignity and (2) risking the appearance of cowardice."[21]

While Morrison warned shortly after the presidential election that the nation was heading in a disastrous direction, the US Conference of Catholic Bishops announced in August 2017 that it was launching a new committee to address racism, reportedly the US Catholic Church's first serious attempt to tackle the issue since 1979. The same month that the American Catholic hierarchy formed its antiracism ad hoc committee, news broke that William Aitcheson, a white priest from Arlington, Virginia, formerly belonged to the Ku Klux Klan and had been arrested for terrorizing Black and Jewish families in the 1970s. Incredibly, he'd never formally apologized for these acts of racial terrorism or made concrete efforts to help the victims heal, angering African Americans both in and outside Catholic communities. The next year, the US Conference of Catholic Bishops drafted a statement condemning racism and expressing their intention to fight it, but some Black Catholics said those remarks did not hold the church accountable for its role in slavery and segregation. The institution had enslaved African Americans in multiple states and enforced Jim Crow in parishes, schools, convents, hospitals, and seminaries. Given this history, Black Catholics argued that mere words opposing racism would not serve as sufficient recompense.

Today, Black Catholics remain on the periphery of the church, with African Americans making up fewer than 1 percent of all priests (or 250 out of 36,500 total) and about 3.2 percent of all bishops (or 8 out of more than 250 total).[22] In October 2020, Pope Francis's announcement of thirteen new cardinals drew an unusual amount of interest because the list included Washington, DC, archbishop Wilton Gregory, the first African American to serve in the role.

It's unclear how Morrison managed being a minority in the Catholic Church or how her relationship with the institution evolved over time. "Since Morrison has been less forthright than others about her lived Catholic practice after her conversion, I tend to view her like I do the late Robert Stone—as someone whose work is suffused with Catholic faith, culture, and ritual, but who would be best understood as a 'cultural Catholic' rather than a practicing Catholic writer," Ripatrazone told me in 2017.[23]

The Christianity in her work can be seen in how she explored themes of death and rebirth in *Song of Solomon*, *Beloved*, and *Paradise*, all novels in which characters manage to live after death through supernatural means. It is also found in the redemption arcs she gave her characters. They may be deeply flawed people, but Morrison did not condemn them for their mistakes. She charted their journey to personal and spiritual growth, much like readers of the Bible see the miraculous transformation and conversion of Saul from persecutor of Christians to champion of the faith. "The search is always more important than the conclusion, and at times the conclusion is in the journey," she said.[24]

While Morrison revealed very little about her faith life publicly, she told NPR in 2016 that she'd taken her religion "seriously for years and years and years."[25] At some point, she began to drift away from Catholicism and to take a more scholarly approach to the Bible. She noted how the Scriptures have "gone through so many hands, so many translations," not to mention the countless changes scribes made to them. Knowing about these alterations caused her to regard the Bible as "an interesting project," more so than the exact word of God. Still, Morrison acknowledged that she hadn't necessarily put her church days behind her. "I might be easily seduced to go back to church because I like the controversy as well as the beauty of this particular Pope Francis," she said. "He's very interesting to me."[26]

Pope Francis stands out for his outspokenness against xenophobia, religious persecution, and racism. After the May 25, 2020, Minneapolis police killing of African American George Floyd set off international protests, he remarked, "We cannot close our eyes to any form of racism or exclusion while pretending to defend the sacredness of every human life."[27] The pope has also called for governments to treat migrants and refugees with humanity and intimated that women who've had abortions and gay people don't deserve public condemnation (though he has yet to allow the church to bless same-sex unions). And well before the movement to abolish the police made national headlines in 2020, he even criticized mass incarceration, noting in 2014 that the most marginalized people in society all too often fill the prisons.

The marginalized fill the pages of Morrison's books. Orphans, battered women, rape victims, single mothers, shell-shocked soldiers, and people with physical and mental disabilities are among the many characters who populate her fiction. In this way, she used her writing to emulate Christ's outreach to the vulnerable, a group Pope Francis is championing through his frankness on social issues and consistent compassion for the oppressed. Arguably history's most liberal pontiff, Francis has also distinguished himself by not downplaying the need for liberation theology. Born and raised in Argentina, Francis saw first-hand the impact of liberation theology in Latin America and recalled during a 2019 gathering with thirty Central American Jesuits that he had once met Father Gustavo Gutiérrez, the Peruvian theologian who spearheaded the movement. Francis has even made a point to send public birthday wishes to Gutiérrez, a move his predecessors likely would not have made.

"During the 1980s, the Vatican's doctrinal office under then-Cardinal Joseph Ratzinger, the future Pope Benedict XVI, issued two major documents on liberation theology, praising the movement's concern for the poor and for justice, but condemning a tendency to rely too heavily on Marxist social analysis," according to the Catholic News Service.[28]

As Pope Francis met with the group of Central American Jesuits in 2019, he discussed how Jesuits from that region had played a fundamental role in the Catholic social justice movement, the architects of which he said sometimes made mistakes. But, he added, so had the Catholic Church leaders who had been quick to condemn liberation theology while tacitly supporting oppressive regimes.

The Catholic hierarchy's opposition to liberation theology continued well into the 2010s. Pope Francis described how he was told that canonizing Óscar Arnulfo Romero, the fourth archbishop of San Salvador, would be "like canonizing Marxism,"[29] as Romero was known for criticizing the political forces that had fostered economic and social injustice, torture, and assassinations in El Salvador during the period before that nation's civil war. For speaking out against oppression, Romero was assassinated in 1980, but Francis didn't deem Romero too political for sainthood. Instead, he canonized the archbishop in October 2018.

Due to Pope Francis's unyielding support of society's rebels, outcasts, and downtrodden, it's clear why Morrison took an interest in him, since she used her writing to humanize and advocate for the oppressed. What's less evident is why Morrison, a self-described champion for Blackness, devoted herself to a religious institution in the United States with a small African American following and a history of anti-Black racism. Remaining in her mother's beloved AME Church, which has focused on Black liberation since its inception, would have seemingly been the more radical choice. But *Authentically Black and Truly Catholic* author Cressler points out that while Black Catholics aren't the norm in the United States, they are the norm in the Western hemisphere, where most Black Christians are Catholic and most Catholics are people of color. Since Black Christians have for centuries been religiously diverse rather than exclusively Protestant, Morrison's Catholic conversion connected her to Catholics of African descent throughout the Americas.

A Historic Black Catholic Presence

The Black Catholics in Morrison's fiction hail from both North and South America—from the Gulf Coast of the United States in *Sula* to the shores of Brazil in *Paradise*. Morrison, then, was interested not just in diasporic Africans but in Catholic diasporic Africans. The presence of Black Catholics in the Americas goes back as far as the earliest days of colonization. Esteban the Moor, also known as "Black Stephen," was an enslaved Moroccan Catholic explorer who survived Spanish conquistador Pánfilo de Narváez's 1527 expedition to colonize Florida after storms left the crew shipwrecked and many dead near the Texas coast. Since Esteban was enslaved and Spain required the explorers it sent to the Americas to be Catholic, it's not clear how much of a say he had in his conversion, but he might have been the first Black Catholic to set foot in this region.

Two hundred years afterward, in 1739, Catholics with ethnic origins in central Africa's Kingdom of Kongo were among the enslaved South Carolinians who took part in an uprising against their captors that's now known as the Stono Rebellion. The revolt started on the feast day commemorating the nativity of the Virgin Mary and is the largest rebellion by enslaved people to occur in the thirteen colonies prior to the Revolutionary War. During their uprising, these freedom fighters drew upon their Catholicism, especially their belief that Mary would intercede on their behalf for God's deliverance. In Morrison's *Paradise*, the Madonna emerges as a central maternal figure in the text, one that delivers the orphaned protagonist Consolata Sosa from a life of anguish and nurtures her as she has nurtured countless others.

Although they were enslaved, the Kongolese who participated in the Stono Rebellion weren't converts via colonization; instead, they were "cradle Catholics who for generations learned the faith from their own people with a devotion to Mary that rivals that of Mexico or Poland," *U.S. Catholic* magazine reported.[30] Catholicism spread in the Kingdom of Kongo in 1491 when King João I became a believer after interacting with Portuguese missionaries. But João "resisted Portuguese colonialism and established direct relations with Rome," the magazine elaborated. "Under the 'Constantine of the Congo,' the nation developed its own school and catechetical system. By the 17th century, the capital was an episcopal see with a cathedral and 12 churches."[31]

The Kongolese were particularly devoted to Mary, whom they called *Mamanzambi*, or "Mother of God." They sang the rosary in the Kikongo language, the hymn "Stella Caeli Extirpavit" in Latin, and left offerings for Mary each Saturday, their Sabbath. The Kongolese believed that Mary protected them, and they turned to her when tragedy, conflict, or drought struck, just as Morrison's characters often reach out to the holy women in their communities during times of crisis.

The Kongolese enslaved in South Carolina remained steadfast Catholics even though the colony did not get a Catholic priest until 1786. And their faith contributed to the decision of twenty-three Kongolese to run away to Florida in 1738, the year before the Stono Rebellion. Catholic priests in Florida sent word that they could live as free people in the city of St. Augustine, named after the fourth-century theologian who Black Catholics often invoke to argue that Catholicism is rightfully their religion. A North African of Amazigh heritage, St. Augustine has been recognized as a doctor of the church or as a saint who made key contributions to Catholic doctrine. The North African's shaping of the church has given Black people a sense of Catholic ownership they might not otherwise have.

Arguing that Morrison employed a Catholic womanist theology in her literature makes it important to recognize the historic African ties to Catholicism and the outsized role that Mary played in this development. By choice rather than by force, people of African descent left their imprint on the religion and adopted it as their own. Reminiscent of the mother goddesses in African indigenous religions, the Blessed Virgin emerged as a major reason Africans felt drawn to Catholicism. For centuries, diasporic Africans have viewed Mary as a liberating force, a tradition Morrison continued in books such as *Paradise*.

In the end, the Virgin Mary didn't intercede for South Carolina's rebel Kongolese Catholics, who were killed by their oppressors, but that didn't stop Black Americans from practicing Catholicism. St. Augustine Church, the oldest parish established by African Americans, dates back to 1841 in racially diverse New Orleans. When the church first opened, its congregation was about a third white, a third free people of color, and a third enslaved African American.

"While there were free Blacks all over the slaveholding South before the Civil War, the free people of color in New Orleans were unique," according to the *National Catholic Reporter.* "Many were the offspring of French and Black parents; some came from French colonial holdings in the Caribbean. They had French names, and some had been educated in Europe. Most importantly, they were Catholic."[32]

Advocates for the poor and the oppressed would play important roles at St. Augustine, including parishioners such as Henriette Delille, a free woman of color born in 1813 who was dedicated to serving and teaching the needy, be they liberated or enslaved. Although she could have passed for white, as many of her family members had, she established an order of Black nuns called the Sisters of the Holy Family that continues today. Delille has recently become the subject of numerous articles and research papers, as she is on the path to becoming the first African American saint after Pope Benedict XVI declared her venerable in 2010.

Nuns were a subject of particular interest for Morrison. In *The Bluest Eye*, the narrator mentions these holy women in a passing reference—"Nuns go by quiet as lust, and drunken men and sober eyes sing in the lobby of the Greek hotel."[33] Twenty-seven years later, Morrison made a convent the central focus of *Paradise*.

In addition to Henriette Delille, St. Augustine's notable parishioners include civil rights activists Homer Plessy and A. P. Tureaud Sr. Just one-eighth African American, Plessy fought racial segregation laws by boarding the white section of a train just blocks away from St. Augustine. His admission to a train worker that he was a man of color led to his arrest, and his case made it all the way to the

US Supreme Court, which ruled in 1896 that "separate but equal" laws weren't unconstitutional. That decision would be reversed in the 1954 Supreme Court case *Brown v. Board of Education*.

Tureaud was born three years after the *Plessy* decision and would go on to become a civil rights activist, teaming up with Thurgood Marshall to strike down Jim Crow laws. Marshall, of course, was the plaintiff's attorney in the *Brown v. Board* case and later would become the first African American to serve on the Supreme Court. That activists such as Plessy and Tureaud came out of St. Augustine Church illustrates that Black Protestant churches weren't the only ones that contributed to the civil rights movement. Catholic churches were an important source of African American activism as well.

While St. Augustine was home to important racial justice activists, it wasn't free from racism. In the 1950s, it enforced segregation in the sanctuary, requiring Black parishioners to sit in the last three pews of the church and to receive Communion after white parishioners did. Moreover, after Catholic schools in the city were racially integrated in 1962, white New Orleanians fled in droves, and St. Augustine became a mostly African American church. Because Lorain, Ohio, was racially integrated, Morrison likely didn't experience this kind of division in Catholic churches during her youth there in the 1940s. (As a student, and later a teacher, at Howard University in Washington, DC, she very well could have encountered racial discrimination in church because her higher education marked her first opportunity to venture into the South.) Today, St. Augustine's Jim Crow past appears to be very much over, although not forgotten by the elders who lived through the period. As of 2021, a Zambian man, Father Emmanuel Mulenga, leads the church as part of his first US parish assignment.

From Esteban the Moor to St. Augustine's most celebrated Black members, African American Catholics have a long and complicated history. They have fought against racial injustice and been subjected to it by the church. Yet for centuries, people of African descent have embraced Catholicism. Beyond a devout cousin and a fascination with rituals, Toni Morrison never revealed what drew her to the faith, once admitting that as a girl, she felt "perfectly content with its aesthetics." As a woman who believed in magic, centered the divine feminine in her literature, and wrote for Black readers, her attraction to Catholicism makes perfect sense. It is, after all, a belief system where miracles are accepted and the Virgin Mary is venerated. And it easily lends itself to syncretism, allowing diasporic Africans to weave their indigenous spirituality within the religion. In *Paradise*, Morrison explored this syncretism in detail, focusing on the Afro-Brazilian religion of Candomblé, which blends Yoruba spirituality with Roman Catholicism.

Syncretism, Magic, and the Divine Feminine

In Morrison's literature, people fly, resurrect the dead, and foretell the future. Ghosts return to comfort—and sometimes terrorize—their loved ones. The amazing occurrences that take place in her fiction don't particularly surprise her characters because in the African worldview, miracles are possible, just as they are in the Catholic cosmology.

The small Italian town of Carmiano, Lecce, is a case in point. In August 2020, it made global headlines because Catholic locals swore that a miracle had occurred there: a statue of the Virgin Mary, built seventy-seven years earlier in the Paolino Arnesano Square, was weeping blood. Braving stifling heat and the novel coronavirus, mobs flocked to the statue as word spread about the fantastic sight, which had also been captured on video. Was it a hoax or truly a miracle?

Father Riccardo Calabrese of the Sant'Antonio Abate Church in Pisa said that he was unclear if the statue was crying blood as the result of a miracle or torrid temperatures or if the entire spectacle was "someone's idea of a joke."[34] In any case, the bishop of Lecce announced that the Catholic Church would investigate the claims that a miracle had taken place. It wouldn't be the first time. Catholics have claimed for centuries that statues of the Blessed Virgin inexplicably began to weep, that they saw an apparition of Mary, or that she provided supernatural aid to them during a time of crisis, just as the protagonist of *Paradise* provides supernatural help to those in need. According to Mathew Schmalz, a College of the Holy Cross religion professor, "Throughout Catholic history, supernatural events have been attributed to Mary's power. When France's Chartres cathedral burned, only Mary's relic—called 'The Veil of the Virgin'—survived after being safeguarded by three priests who were miraculously preserved from the heat and flames. Mary's intercession is also believed to have ensured victory at the Battle of Lepanto in 1571, when an Ottoman fleet was repulsed by the forces of Genoa, Venice and the papacy."[35]

When Mary weeps, she does so because of "the sins of the world" and the emotional distress she experienced in life, Schmalz explained. This grief is known as "the seven sorrows of Mary" or "the seven dolors of Mary," and it includes her temporary loss of the boy Jesus, the death and crucifixion of Jesus, the taking of his body, and his burial. The image of seven swords puncturing Mary's heart, sometimes depicted on fire, represents her sorrows. Women in mourning appear throughout Morrison's works, a pattern that dates back to her earliest fiction, particularly *Sula* and *Song of Solomon*. Like Mary, they grieve their dead children, but they muster the wherewithal to keep on going. After losing her son to cancer in 2010, Morrison found herself among these grieving mothers. She also grieved, as Mary did, about "what's going on in the world."[36]

When Mary sculptures cry, often some kind of deceit is responsible for the event, such as when a statue of her in Forlì, Italy, reportedly wept blood in 2006.[37] The blood, though, turned out to belong to a church custodian who was later tried for the fraudulent act. In other instances, liquids have been deposited into statues to make them cry. The eyes of statues can also be treated with a combination of oil and fat to produce tears when temperatures begin to soar in sanctuaries. Sometimes, no cause for the tears is identified, but the common thread in all these cases is that the Catholic Church takes them seriously enough to investigate them, and congregants have a strong desire to believe in their legitimacy. Throngs of Catholics have made pilgrimages to see these "weeping" statues in person. For example, in Carmiano, Lecce, Father Calabrese said he "saw a procession of people who, out of curiosity or faith, left their homes to gather there."[38]

Just like "Black people believe in magic,"[39] as Morrison asserted, Catholics believe in miracles. And as a Black Catholic writer, miracles and magic define her work. In *The Bluest Eye*, the magic is found in the women healers and seers, and the miracle is found in the tragic little Black girl at its center who believes she has been granted blue eyes. Morrison ended her career with another tragic little Black girl, Bride, the heroine of *God Help the Child*. A beautiful and successful career woman as an adult, Bride magically reverts back into her prepubescent body to grapple with her inner child. The miracle of the book is that after a childhood of abuse and abandonment, Bride is able to create a loving family of her own.

The culture around miracles distinguishes Catholicism from Protestantism, a branch of Christianity in which miracles aren't attributed to the Virgin Mary or to other saints. While Protestants believe in the miracles of Jesus and that God is capable of miraculous feats like healing the sick, mainline Protestant churches don't place the same emphasis on miracles in contemporary society that the Catholic Church does. In short, Catholics are overwhelmingly interested in what Morrison described as "the strange stuff."[40]

According to historian and anthropologist Davíd Carrasco, whom Morrison consulted about Afro-Brazilian religions while writing *Paradise*, she considered "the strange stuff" to be a vital "part of the religion in [her] work."[41]

Her Catholicism, a belief system in which miracles are not just relegated to antiquity but accepted as part of life today, surely informed this religious view—as did her Blackness. In the lives of her characters, she pointed out, "birds talk and butterflies cry, and it is not surprising or upsetting to them." Such magical events unfold in her novels to reflect the "vast imagination of Black people" who existed in Morrison's personal orbit. These individuals didn't just recite folklore; they believed in the stories they told, even the ones about Africans who could fly.

"I don't care how silly it may seem," Morrison said of that folktale. "It is everywhere—people used to talk about it; it's in the spirituals and gospels. Perhaps it was wishful thinking—escape, death, and all that. But suppose it wasn't. What might it mean?"[42]

Similarly, the Catholic Church investigates tales of weeping Virgin Mary statues. Sure, these reports might be hoaxes, and often are, but if not, what might they mean? What message does Mary want to communicate? The church's acknowledgment that mysterious events can and do happen dovetails with African traditional religions that likewise recognize the importance of the inexplicable. This shared sense of how the world functions contributed to the Catholicization of the Kingdom of Kongo.

While scholars believe that the hope of political and economic gain, especially the establishment of Portugal as a trade partner, factored into the Catholic conversion of Kongo's King João, this wasn't necessarily the case for his son Afonso I. João eventually cooled to Catholicism, but Afonso, who reigned from roughly 1506 to 1543, appeared to be an enthusiastic believer. He spent years studying with Portuguese priests and eventually established the Roman Catholic Church of Kongo. He even credited his ascension to the throne to a miracle of Catholic proportions. After João's death, Afonso's half brother, Mpanzu a Kitima, fought him for control of the Kingdom of Kongo, assembling a large army to thwart his sibling. Although Afonso did not have nearly as many soldiers as his brother did, he claimed that he managed to win the battle after the ghost of Saint James the Great appeared in the sky and scared Mpanzu's forces away.

Afonso Henriques, the early Portuguese king who ruled from 1139 to 1185, clearly inspired this story.[43] During his victorious 1139 battle against the Almoravids, an Amazigh dynasty, he claimed to have seen Saint James and the cross of Constantine. After Afonso of Kongo experienced the same "miracle" in similar circumstances, the Kingdom of Kongo, which spanned more than 115,000 square miles, became a Catholic empire. With elements of syncretism, Kongolese Catholicism wasn't a mere facsimile of European Catholicism. According to the Metropolitan Museum of Art, "The translations of Christian doctrine into the local language, Kikongo, were done such that words like *spirit*, *god*, and *holy* were rendered directly equivalent to existing concepts in Kongo cosmology. Missionary documents from the 17th century claimed that they had found a people who believed in a single god but did not know his name. . . . In parts of Kongo, Christianity was accepted not as a new religion that would replace the old but rather as a new syncretic cult that was fully compatible with existing structures."[44]

In *Paradise*, a "syncretic cult" that merges West African spirituality with Roman Catholicism inspires the hatred of outsiders who brand such a belief system evil, but the Kingdom of Kongo demonstrates how Africans have approached religion in this way for centuries, if not always. Afonso and his team built churches in spaces that the Kongolese already considered sacred, and they linked Catholic saints to divine entities in Kongo cultures. Whether or not they became Catholics as free people, diasporic Africans would engage in this kind of syncretism. The fact that Catholicism includes saints, human beings so exceptional that they are deemed holy in death, parallels the widespread ancestor worship in African religious cultures. The veneration of one saint in particular, Mary, mother of God, has long made Black people curious about the Catholic Church.

Like many Catholics, the Kongolese viewed Mary as their protector, but paintings of her as the Black Madonna dating back to antiquity have particularly drawn Black people to Catholicism. Morrison's literature, which references a multicolored Madonna in *Sula* and one as dark as firewood in *Paradise*, reveals that she also took an interest in the Dark Virgin. Some scholars attribute the dark color of these Madonnas to centuries of burning candles in churches or an equally long accumulation of dirt and grime. Others say that artists intentionally painted Black Madonnas because the Dark Virgin was a Christian adaptation of ancient earth goddesses typically depicted as dark skinned.[45] Goddesses like Artemis, Isis, and Ceres were portrayed as Black because "the best fertile soil is black in color and the blacker it is, the more suited it is for agriculture," according to Michael

Duricy of the International Marian Research Institute at the University of Dayton. Additionally, art historians assert that depictions of the Dark Virgin reflect the following line in the *Song of Solomon* spoken by the bride: "I am black but beautiful."[46] And in communities where the natives have dark skin, be it in Africa or Latin America, Mary is dark to reflect the Indigenous populations there.

No matter the origins of the Black Madonna, diasporic Africans have recognized themselves in depictions of her. The most famous Dark Virgin is arguably Poland's Black Madonna of Częstochowa, which Pope Clement XI granted a canonical coronation in 1717.[47] Haitian Vodou practitioners went on to adopt Poland's Black Madonna as the image of the loa, or spirit, known as Ezilí Dantor.[48] She became the patron saint of the Haitian Revolution after Polish soldiers joined forces with the Haitian rebels fighting French rule of their land.

Since Catholicism has recognized images of the divine Black feminine, it appeals to the Black community in ways that Protestantism does not. Although Morrison did not attach her decision to become a Catholic (and remain one for years) to this aspect of the institution, it is readily apparent that the divine Black feminine was a concept that fascinated her. From her first novel to her last, she explored the godliness of Black women and the damage that results when they are dehumanized and denigrated, their divinity denied to them.

4

Sula's Deconstruction of the Madonna, the Whore, and the Witch

Toni Morrison's *Sula* has widely been described as a novel about betrayal's impact on the friendship between two Black women. The book certainly explores this issue but does not stop there. It uses the friendship between Sula Peace and Nel Wright to examine morality and its role in both the community and the individual, making it one of Morrison's most religious texts. The novel not only asks what makes a person good and what makes one evil; it also blurs the line between these concepts and suggests that society benefits from both. Remove the evil from a community and watch it crumble, *Sula* contends.

While the Bible doesn't explicitly make this case, Morrison used the novel to explore how communities have historically drawn on the fallen angel Satan and the human evil he personifies to vilify and dehumanize others. More specifically, *Sula* engages the biblical concept of the scapegoat, which derives from the Levitican ceremony that saw the Israelites project all their sins onto an "escape goat" released into the wilderness to symbolically remove the iniquity from their ranks.

In her investigation of good and evil, Morrison fills *Sula* with other dualities, including the hills and the valley, order and disorder, fire and ice, sanity and insanity. Set from 1919 to 1965, *Sula* considers how women's sexuality has historically been weaponized to frame them as good or bad by deconstructing the Madonna-whore dichotomy. Nel Wright views herself as good because she's a devoted mother and wife, while child-free Sula Peace is branded evil largely because she has indiscriminate sex with all sorts of men—Black and white, married and single—in her small Ohio town. The very different ways these women approach sex ultimately drive them apart.

That Morrison made one of these characters a "virgin" and the other a "whore," only to go on to declare these women indistinguishable from each other, points to both her Catholic sensibilities and her womanist instincts that resent the patriarchy's impact on female sexuality. A 2018 research study about the Madonna-whore complex described the dichotomy as follows:

> In Camerino's (c. 1400) painting, *The Madonna of Humility with the Temptation of Eve*, the Virgin Mary—representing

chastity and purity—holds the infant Jesus, while below Eve lies naked with a serpent and fur around her hips and legs, representing sexual lust and temptation. Polarized representations of women in general as either good (chaste and pure) Madonnas or bad (promiscuous and seductive) whores can be traced from the ancient Greeks through later Western literature, art, as well as contemporary films and television series. Still prevalent in the West, this dichotomy also occurs in non-Western cultures—in Latin and South America in the Middle East and East Asia—where female chastity is integral to family honor.[1]

It also occurs in Africa, where many countries skew heavily Christian or Muslim. In some parts of the continent, female genital mutilation (alternatively known as female circumcision) has traditionally been practiced to control female sexuality. Since this procedure typically entails removing some or all of the clitoris, a female sex organ that helps women climax, it is performed in part to reduce sexual temptation. Given that female circumcision lends women who have endured it an air of respectability, the practice is said to improve a woman's marriage prospects as well. Now considered a human rights issue, countries throughout Africa have banned this custom, but it is still performed clandestinely in some areas.

In the United States, the legacy of slavery has complicated sexuality for Black women. Raped by the men who enslaved them, forced to breed with others in bondage, and denied the legal right to marry, they could not choose to be "good," chaste women who waited until marriage to have intercourse. The sexual violence Black women endured during captivity is documented in slave narratives such as *Incidents in the Life of a Slave Girl* and *Louisa Picquet, the Octoroon, or, Inside Views of Southern Domestic Life.* After slavery, white men could still rape the Black women who worked in their homes as domestic servants or who lived in their communities without fear of punishment. In 1931, future civil rights champion Rosa Parks survived an attempted rape while working as a maid in a white household. "I was ready to die," she wrote in a letter about the incident, "but give my consent, never. Never, never. . . . If he wanted to kill me and rape a dead body, he was welcome, but he would have to kill me first."[2]

The dehumanization that Black women experienced during slavery and Jim Crow made them vulnerable to sexual predators, but this didn't mean that African Americans disregarded concepts such as virginity and virtue. The Black women who wrote slave narratives about being held in bondage by licentious white men very much emphasized that chastity and matrimony mattered to them, as they did to heavily religious African Americans during and after slavery. Even in captivity, robbed of their humanity and their right to marry, Black couples engaged in rituals such as jumping the broom to declare their lifelong commitment to each other. When slavery ended, educated and elite Black Americans did not hesitate to show society that the men and women among them were every bit as respectable as their white counterparts. And for women, respectability meant abstinence until marriage. Challenging a white racist ideology that characterized Black women as sexually promiscuous and animalistic—and therefore "unrapable"—was an act of resistance.

In the Sundown House's Shadow

For *Sula*'s Helene Sabat, mother of Nel Wright, virginity was a source of impeccability. It also drew a distinct line between her and her estranged Creole mother, Rochelle, a sex worker at the Sundown House in New Orleans. The narrator explains early on that the Sundown's red shutters have haunted Helene since she was born there and that she is grateful to her grandmother, Cecile, for rescuing her from a childhood in a whorehouse. In contrast, Cecile raises her "under the dolesome eyes of a multicolored Virgin Mary, counseling her to be constantly on guard for any sign of her mother's wild blood."[3]

Setting portions of *Sula* in a city with both a rich Black Catholic tradition and a reputation for vice enabled Morrison to engage the Madonna-whore dichotomy more explicitly than she could have if the novel had exclusively taken place in fictional Medallion, Ohio. Helene and Rochelle (along with Cecile and Rochelle) make up the first Madonna-whore pair presented in *Sula*. The Virgin Mary who watches over Helene is not white but "multicolored," a sort of Black Madonna. Multicolored due to her Creole heritage, Cecile reveres a Blessed Virgin whom she resembles. Her Catholicism, then, does not parrot white Catholicism, but her belief that Rochelle has "wild blood" is very much a white supremacist construct stemming from the enslavement of African Americans and the miscegenation that accompanied it.

Mixed-race women were historically characterized as Jezebels, or seductresses, to absolve the white men who enslaved and sexually assaulted them of blame for their egregious abuses of power. In the Bible, Jezebel was the beautiful but devious wife of the seventh king of Israel, Ahab. She promoted idol worship and used her feminine wiles to execute evil schemes before meeting a terrible end that saw dogs devour her carcass. Ironically, her name, which means "chaste, free from carnal connection," is now a colloquialism to describe wicked women generally.[4]

When white society was not framing Black women as Jezebels, it was characterizing them as "mammies." Dark skinned and heavyset, the mammy was a nonsexual being who found fulfillment in taking care of white families. Unlike the Virgin Mary, her maternity was not worshipped, for the mammy existed solely to serve white people. Morrison engages the mammy archetype in *The Bluest Eye*, as Pecola Breedlove's mother finds purpose in caring for the white family who employs her, but she deprives her own child of motherly affection and protection.

Both the Jezebel and the mammy archetypes functioned to subdue Black women, and the former role in particular perpetuated their sexual exploitation. If having Black blood made one an inherently "wild" Jezebel, white men could not be held responsible for raping them. As Ferris University sociologist David Pilgrim explains, "The mulatto approximated the white ideal of female attractiveness. All slave women (and men and children) were vulnerable to being raped, but the mulatto afforded the slave owner the opportunity to rape, with impunity, a woman who was physically white (or near-white) but legally Black."[5]

During and after enslavement, miscegenation laws prevented free people of color from marrying their white partners, and in cities such as New Orleans, multiracial women sometimes had common-law marriages with white men who would financially support them and any children their unions produced—a system known as *plaçage*. Henriette Delille, the nineteenth-century free woman of color now up for sainthood, reportedly entered into such an arrangement with a white man before devoting herself to the church. Some historians dispute that *plaçage* occurred as frequently in New Orleans as the public has been led to believe or that wealthy white men essentially purchased mixed-race women at "quadroon balls." Emily Clark, a historian at Tulane University, told New Orleans Public Radio in 2016 that free women of color were among the city's most pious during the colonial period and to characterize them as concubines ignores that reality. Clark asserts, "We rob them of having attained the ideal of being a lady when we erase their story and instead accept what was the story told about all Black women which was that it's not the white man's fault that they go to bed with Black women, and even that they rape them. It's the woman's fault because they are so seductive. . . . When we buy this myth, we're buying into that really old and I think socially destructive and just plain not historically accurate idea about women of African descent."[6]

It would be an overstatement to say that Morrison bought into this myth when she made Rochelle a sex worker. Since this character is not given a backstory, it's unclear why she became involved in the sex trade, a significant omission considering that Cecile objects to her lifestyle and becomes Helene's caregiver. These details suggest that Rochelle didn't become a prostitute because she had no family support or because desperation drove her into the profession; perhaps she just gravitated toward the work. Additionally, her abandonment of Helene points to a character deficit, but the fact that Morrison highlights the (outward) piety of both Cecile and Helene makes it clear that she's not painting all Creole women with a broad brush. Mainly, she frames Rochelle as a foil for Helene and the reason Helene is so uptight and controlling when she marries Wiley Wright and moves from New Orleans to Medallion to escape her past.

In Ohio, Helene—whose maiden name of Sabat connects her to the Holy Sabbath—looks for the most conservative Black church she can find, since Medallion doesn't have a Catholic parish. She tries to mold Nel into a miniature version of herself, raising her daughter to be obedient, polite, and devoid of all passion. As the narrator notes, "Any enthusiasms that little Nel showed were calmed by the mother until she drove her daughter's imagination underground."[7]

But a trip to New Orleans after Cecile dies makes it clear that Nel is her own person. In her great-grandmother's house, the child sees paintings of the Virgin Mary with clasped hands "three times in the front room and once in the bedroom where Cecile's body lay."[8] Nel, though, isn't drawn to the Blessed Virgin; she's drawn to Rochelle, smelling of gardenias and dressed in canary yellow for a somber occasion that customarily calls for black. The narrator characterizes Rochelle as both angelic—her hair is in a "halo-like roll"—and a bit of a witch.[9] Without flinching, she strikes a match, extinguishes it, and darkens her eyebrows "with the burnt head."[10] While heat so close to the face would make most people reflexively shrink back, the warmth does not faze Rochelle, one reason she appears so mysterious to young Nel.

The little girl marvels at her forty-eight-year-old grandmother and wants to understand the dialect that she speaks, but Helene is clear that no daughter of hers will speak Creole. She denies speaking it herself despite communicating with Rochelle in the language right in front of Nel. Although a segregated train ride to New Orleans demonstrates that adopting white cultural norms will never make white people view her as their equal—she's called "gal" during the trip and forced to urinate outside—Helene rejects her Creole roots and her daughter's broad nose. When they return to Medallion, she instructs her daughter to hold her nose in hopes of making it more aquiline and European looking, ignoring Nel's complaint that doing so hurts. Outwardly, Nel grudgingly obeys her mother, but inwardly, she vows to be her own woman. Her audacious grandmother has inspired her to individuate from Helene, and her first act of rebellion is to befriend Sula Peace, a classmate Helene disapproves of because "her mother was sooty."[11] It's not clear if the sootiness in question refers to skin color or character, but given Helene's snobbishness and distaste for overtly Black features, both likely apply.

A Friendship Forged in Trauma

When Helene gets to know Sula, she's pleasantly surprised that "she seemed to have none of her mother's slackness."[12] And Sula loves the immaculate furnishings in the Wright household, which Nel has always found oppressively orderly. Meanwhile, Nel falls in love with how different Sula's upbringing is from her own. Instead of a nuclear family, Sula lives with her mother, grandmother, and the "villagers" they have taken into their household, where dirty dishes accumulate in the sink and extra staircases add to the chaos. Sula's grandmother Eva has just one leg and hands Nel "goobers from deep inside her pockets" and "reads" dreams—a detail that hints at her divinity.[13] Eva is very much like Morrison's own grandmother, a storyteller who interpreted dreams, but the tales Eva spins never quite explain the reason for her missing limb:

> Unless Eva herself introduced the subject, no one ever spoke of her disability; they pretended to ignore it, unless, in some mood of fancy, she began some fearful story about it—generally to entertain children. How the leg got up by itself one day and walked on off. How she hobbled after it but it ran too fast, Or how she had a corn on her toe and it just grew and grew until her whole foot was a corn and then it traveled on up her leg and wouldn't stop growing until she put a red rag at the top but by that time it was already at her knee.[14]

Like Blue Jack of *The Bluest Eye*, who told Cholly Breedlove a strange story about the ghost of a headless white woman crying for a comb, Eva has a penchant for the fantastic. The reality, the narrator hints, is that she intentionally injured herself after her husband left her alone with three children and no money with which to raise them. In desperation, she allowed a train to run over her leg and got a cash settlement she used to care for her children and build a new house in the hills of the Black community ironically known as the Bottom. The extreme sacrifice this self-sufficient Black woman makes is an example of womanist Christology. As womanists do, she sought to improve her family's circumstances, but her willingness to put her life on the line to change their plight likens her to Jesus Christ. Morrison also draws attention to Eva's divinity by situating her residence in a sparsely populated area of the Bottom, just as *The Bluest Eye*'s M'Dear lives in a shack near the woods and the other holy women in Morrison's fiction live on the outskirts of town. While M'Dear is a healer, Eva is more of a village mother and caregiver who takes in human strays and can remedy her children's medical ailments if necessary. Unlike M'Dear, Eva is described as having sex appeal and wearing clothing that accentuates the one comely leg she has left.

All the women in Eva's family crave the company of men, which stands in stark contrast to Helene Wright, who enjoys her husband's long work-related absences from home and took nine years to have her only child, Nel, a detail the narrator includes to suggest that she and Wiley have sex infrequently. Once Nel comes along, Helene clearly prefers the role of mother to that of wife. She is Madonna-like, while the Peace women appear to be Eve-like, indulging in their sexuality. Eva's name emphasizes her connection to the Garden of Eden's fallen woman, but Morrison shows that the Peace family matriarch is too complex to cleanly fit into the Eve archetype.

The sacrifices Eva has made for her family show that she's a fierce protector who would go to any length for her children. She has simply managed to integrate her identity as a mother and sexuality as a woman in a way that eludes the novel's other female characters. In Eva, the reader also finds an early prototype of *Beloved*'s Sethe Suggs, who kills her daughter to spare her from a life of slavery. When Eva's son, Plum, returns from World War I shell-shocked and traumatized, she rocks him in her arms and sets him on fire. Eva later explains to her daughter Hannah, Sula's mother, that she killed him to put him out of his misery. In Morrison's literature, filicide is typically not an act that morally depraved parents commit but an act that parents who love their children too much do. With these polar opposite maternal figures, Sula Peace and Nel Wright come of age and find "relief in each other's personality."[15] Ultimately, the killing of another child, a little boy nicknamed Chicken Little, cements Sula and Nel's lifelong bond and reveals each girl's true nature.

Sula and Nel are out playing near the river one day when they encounter the snot-nosed Chicken Little, whom they tease and play with before their fun takes a deadly turn. As Nel swings Chicken around in her hands, she loses her grip, sending him flying into the river and to his death. After the drowning, the twelve-year-olds have completely different reactions to the incident. Sula "collapsed into tears," while Nel's first instinct is to find out if anyone witnessed Chicken's death. She is cool and composed, in contrast to her emotionally fragile friend.[16] Although Sula is wracked with guilt, Nel "knew she had 'done nothing,'" for she isn't the one who swung Chicken into the river and caused him to drown. But neither girl attempts to save him or find someone who could have.[17] In fact, neither Sula nor Nel report his death to anyone, resulting in Chicken's body rotting for three days before it made its way to the embalmer. The little boy's corpse is unrecognizable to all who knew and loved him.

After Chicken's death, Sula is markedly different— "acting up," "dropping things," bothering the boarders in her grandmother's house, and eating food that doesn't belong to her.[18] What's more, "the birthmark over her eye was getting darker and looked more and more like a stem and rose."[19] As the birthmark darkens, Sula becomes more sinister, as if the discolored patch on her face is the mark of the beast in Revelation. Everyone chalks up "Sula's craziness" to the fact that she's going through puberty, but her behavior is more than just a case of haywire hormones.[20] She is grappling with Chicken's death as well as her mother's admission that she loves but does not like her. Hannah's matter-of-fact confession, which Sula accidentally overhears, sends the teen running up to her room in distress. Together, these two events—Chicken's drowning and her mother's dislike of her—change Sula's character. She is beholden to no one but herself.

When Hannah's cotton dress catches on fire after she lights a blaze in the yard, Eva is alarmed to notice that her granddaughter seems indifferent to the fatal mishap, which a dream Hannah had (and Eva interpreted) predicted would occur. Their neighbors, the Suggses, cry out to Jesus and dump water on the fire. Hurting herself in the process, Eva drags her body from the top of the house to the yard to help Hannah—an act of sacrifice that once again frames her as Christlike—and a small crowd gathers near her daughter's burning body in horror. Sula, in contrast, does nothing but stand on the back porch observing the tragedy as it unfolds. The community blames Sula's lack of reaction on the shock of seeing Hannah ablaze, but Eva disagrees—she "remained convinced that Sula had watched Hannah burn not because she was paralyzed, but because she was *interested*."[21] The empathy that made Sula collapse into tears after Chicken's accidental drowning has vanished. The teenager is now a cold individual, and her relationship with Nel stands out as her one significant attachment.

The change in her granddaughter sets Eva on edge, but Nel continues to appreciate Sula's friendship. The girls spend the next five years together closer than ever. And when eighteen-year-old Nel marries a young man named Jude, the narrator explains how she lacks any aggression except for "an occasional leadership role with Sula": "Her parents had succeeded in rubbing down to a dull glow any sparkle or splutter she had. Only with Sula did that quality have free reign [*sic*], but their friendship was so close, they themselves had difficulty distinguishing one's thoughts from the other's. During all of her girlhood the only respite Nel had had from her stern and undemonstrative parents was Sula."[22]

Unaccepted in their families of origin, Sula and Nel form a symbiotic relationship with each other, preventing them from becoming truly autonomous and forming close friendships with a variety of young women. Sula insists that she be Nel's sole bridesmaid, and she's just as happy as Nel is about the nuptials. This isn't because she's such a loving friend. Rather, it's because Sula lacks her own identity, a problem that will lead her to betray Nel.

In Sula, Nel finds a way to access her shadow side, the part of her personality she's been forced to hide growing up with an authoritarian mother who prioritizes conformity, obedience, and respectability over authenticity. Nel is a "good girl" on the outside because Helene has given her no other option. On the inside, though, she's always been drawn to the dark side—starting with her grandmother Rochelle and subsequently Sula.

The Witch Is Back

Initially, Sula's darkness is not evident to the Bottomers, but when she leaves Medallion for a decade following Nel's 1927 wedding, it's clear that she's an ominous force who fits every trope of the witch. The scapegoats of their communities, the women historically labeled witches (though men and children have been branded as such too) typically transgressed gender conventions in some way. They were gifted healers, midwives, and seers, much like the women in Morrison's family, whose talents empowered them in a capacity that struck fear in the ruling class of men. Some became scapegoats because of what they did not do—marry, bear children, or die before their husbands. Others, including the Bible's Jezebel, were branded witches due to the perception that they had flaunted their sexuality or used sex to get ahead. In the book of 2 Kings, Jezebel's son considers that Israel would endure strife "so long as the whoredoms of thy mother Jezebel and her witchcrafts are so many."[23] Whether the women deemed witches were old and withered or young and comely, they shared one commonality: their gender made them vulnerable to persecution. To justify their victimization, their tormentors held them accountable for all manner of tragedies, from disease to disaster.

Morrison revisits the concept of the witch throughout her work, particularly in *Song of Solomon* and *Paradise*, to assert that women aren't evil for refusing to conform to gender norms, but the people bent on punishing such women are indeed morally deficient. Although witches have long been labeled evil, their unjust persecution and the supernatural powers ascribed to them invite comparisons to Christ and, once more, point to Morrison's fascination with the divine feminine. She marks Sula as a witch immediately after the character's arrival in the Bottom. Dressed in dark colors, Sula is unmarried, child-free, and sexually available—and calamity coincides with her return. The narrator notes that she is "accompanied by a plague of robins," a disquieting event that ushers in what the Bottom residents call "evil days."[24]

The glamorous attire Sula wears during her homecoming rivals that of any classic Hollywood villainess and undoubtedly calls the witch to mind. She dons "a black crepe dress splashed with pink and yellow zinnias, foxtails, a black felt hat with the veil of net lowered over one eye."[25] She accessorizes the ensemble with a black purse and an exotic-looking red leather traveling case. Shrouded in mostly black with accoutrements that no one in the Bottom, not even the residents who've traveled abroad, have seen before, Sula is a spectacle when she returns home after her long absence. While some community members greet her, most just stare at her, and others beckon their children back inside at the sight of the woman in black. A witch by any other name, Sula is perceived to be a threat to the neighborhood children.

Having arrived back in town when a plague of birds occurs, she's also a threat to nature. When she makes it to her grandmother's house, she sees four dead robins on the walkway. The grisly scene doesn't make her recoil; she just pushes them onto the bordering grass with the toe of her pump. Setting eyes on her granddaughter for the first time in ten years, Eva quips, "I might have knowed them birds meant something."[26] Eva reads the signs and patterns in the waking world as deftly as she reads dreams, as the African Americans in Morrison's real life did. She knew that it was a bad omen when Hannah dreamed of a red wedding dress, since, in her world, weddings meant death and red meant fire. And she recognized that the dead birds littering the Bottom were not a freak occurrence but, in some way, connected to her granddaughter's return.

Eva views the world much in the same way that Aunt Jimmy's friends in *The Bluest Eye* do. After Jimmy's death, they discuss how they should've known her death was imminent when she asked for black thread. Although Eva is not a medicine woman like *The Bluest Eye*'s M'Dear, her extreme elderliness gives her something in common with the healer of indeterminate old age, like a number of the Bible's patriarchs. By 1937, when Sula returns to Medallion, Eva is well over one hundred years old and has not only the gift of foresight but also the gift of wisdom. She quickly advises Sula to find a husband and have children to get emotionally and spiritually "settled," a tip that makes Sula lash out.

In any other context, this advice could be dismissed as the mundane nagging of an elder who wants to see her granddaughter become a wife and mother. Since witches have long been portrayed as single and childless, Sula's aloneness and insistence that she "wants to make myself" and not "somebody else"[27] signals to the reader why the community regards her with suspicion. They deem independence an unnatural quality in a woman. A woman alone by choice rather than by circumstance is unfamiliar, if not altogether disturbing, to them. Hence Eva advises Sula to settle down so that the village will accept her rather than treat her as an outcast.

But Eva herself is wary of Sula. She doesn't just suspect something's wrong with her grandchild; she's certain of it. When Sula makes a crack about her own mother's premature death and brings up the fact that Eva set Plum on fire, the old woman retorts that Sula's "the one [who] should've been burnt!" and that "hellfire . . . is already burning" in her.[28] In turn, Sula threatens to one day burn up her disabled grandmother, prompting the centenarian to keep her bedroom door locked. It does little good. Sula doesn't kill

Eva but quickly sends her to a nursing home, an affront to the matriarch and to the African American ethos dictating that families take care of their elders. The incident reveals that Sula may not be a witch, but she is certainly capable of causing harm. Even Nel disapproves of Sula sending Eva to Sunnydale, and she's the community member who thinks best of Sula. Having ignored the plague that coincided with Sula's return, Nel associates Sula's homecoming with the magical "rain-soaked Saturday nights" and "lemon-yellow afternoons" that follow the pestilence of birds.[29] Thus both Sula's friend and her foes believe her capable of having supernatural powers. To Nel, Sula is divine, and to the Bottomers, Sula is devilish.

When Nel asks why Sula sent Eva away, Sula frames herself as the victim, accusing her grandmother of making the very threats that she actually made. Nel doubts that Sula feared for her life because of Eva, but she doesn't see her friend as a witch like everyone else does. She views Sula as emotional and irresponsible but delights in how liberated and joyful her friend makes her feel. Nel "alone . . . saw this magic" in Sula, the narrator explains, as the rest of the community recognizes that Sula is an unsafe person.[30] Although Nel notices that the birthmark on her friend's eyelid has grown darker, she doesn't consider it a sign of anything in particular. Raised by a mother who has cut her off from her New Orleans Creole roots, stunted her creativity, and emulated white society, Nel doesn't view the world in the same way that Eva or the other Bottom residents do. Lacking an African-based cosmology, she doesn't make sense of her circumstances by paying attention to signs and patterns, so she fails to notice that Sula's darkened birthmark and implausible explanation for sending Eva away are warnings.

Nel can scarcely believe it when she walks in on her husband, Jude, having sex with Sula, and he proceeds to leave her for her best friend. Disinterested in a relationship with Jude, Sula ditches him to pursue other men, a turn of events that prompts him to relocate to Detroit, permanently breaking up his family. Sula's duplicity involving both Nel and Eva deepens the disgust the Bottom residents already have for her. And her reputation worsens when gossip spreads that Sula sleeps with white men, forever marking her as a Jezebel in the community. The narrator states, "There was nothing lower she could do, nothing filthier. The fact that their own skin color was proof that it had happened in their own families was no deterrent to their bile. Nor was the willingness of Black men to lie in the beds of white women a consideration that might lead them toward tolerance. They insisted that all unions between white men and Black women be rape; for a Black woman to be willing was literally unthinkable. In that way, they regarded integration with precisely the same venom that white people did."[31]

Collectively, the rumor that Sula sleeps with white men and her undisputed treachery against Nel and Eva reinforce the idea that she's a witch. The Bottom residents resort to using conjure, or folk magic, to prevent her from doing more harm to people. They place broomsticks across their doors at night and sprinkle salt on their porch steps to protect themselves from her, yet gossip about Sula's alleged acts of wickedness keeps circulating. Community members blame her for random misfortunes, such as when a five-year-old boy nicknamed Teapot falls and breaks a bone. They also hold her accountable for the choking death of a local man named Mr. Finley, who managed to suck on chicken bones for thirteen years straight without any harm befalling him. When Sula merely looked at Finley, the Bottomers said, he began choking on the spot. The residents also accuse her of "laughing at their God" for showing up to church suppers at establishments like Greater Saint Matthew's without underwear and picking at the food served rather than delighting in anyone's ribs or cobbler.[32] These incidents convince the community that Sula's birthmark represents the ashes of her mother, Hannah, "marking her from the very beginning" as diabolical.[33]

The Bottom community might have even forgiven Sula for one of her sins—her dalliances with married men. Rather than actually take an interest in them, though, she'd sleep with them once and never again, a habit that insulted the men and their wives alike. How dare she suggest that these men were essentially useless—unworthy of a full-blown romantic affair?

Certain that Sula Peace was a cross between a witch and a whore, the Bottom residents mythologize her as a being other than human. They wonder why Sula never had any childhood diseases, still had all her teeth, and lacked rings of fat on her waist or neck despite rapidly approaching thirty. Where were her scars, they wondered, and how come she could drink beer without belching? That made it official, they concluded: Sula "was free of any normal signs of vulnerability."[34] Even Shadrack, the resident "reprobate" in their village, had tipped his hat to her, presumably because one devil recognized another.[35]

"An Artist with No Art Form"

Sula is neither a witch nor a superhuman but a damaged person who has become the neighborhood pariah because she behaves impulsively, transgresses social norms, and lives a fiercely independent existence in a close-knit community with fixed gender roles. She may be a "colored" woman, but she doesn't believe that should stop her from "doing whatever [she] like[s], taking what [she] want[s], leaving what [she] doesn't]."[36] After she falls seriously ill, Sula notes that the difference between her and other Black women is that they're dying like "stumps," while she's "going down like one of those redwoods."[37] Sula says she sure has *lived* in this world, a claim that Nel questions—and not without reason.

In many ways, Sula has spent her short life lashing out in response to unresolved childhood wounds. Her father died young, leaving her in a household where women had one sexual liaison after another without any significant attachment to their lovers. Moreover, her own mother had no emotional attachment to her, "loving" her out of parental obligation only. When Sula accidentally kills Chicken Little, it chips away at what remains of her emotional core. "The first experience [her mother's dislike of her] taught her there was no other that you could count on; the second that there was no self to count on either," the narrator notes. "She had no center, no speck around which to grow."[38]

Instead, Sula spends her decade-long departure away from Medallion flitting from city to city—Nashville, Detroit, New Orleans, New York—and only finds boredom during her travels. Hopping from man to man doesn't help her find the authenticity, friendship, and purpose that can make her whole. Sex doesn't give her pleasure; it just allows her to access the well of pain inside her. She then returns to Medallion in hopes that Nel will fill the void in her life, since in the past, "she had clung to Nel as the closest thing to both an other and a self, only to discover that she and Nel were not one and the same thing."[39] Sula discovers this only after sleeping with Jude to fill the emptiness in her life and devastating Nel in the process. Her best friend does not belong to her anymore, Sula thinks, but to the judgmental town, the residents of which might have been mistaken about the scope and nature of Sula's sins but not altogether wrong about her character deficits.

Today, a woman like Sula might be described as possessing the characteristics commonly found in people with the ten recognized personality disorders. "A personality disorder," according to the American Psychiatric Association, "is a way of thinking, feeling and behaving that deviates from the expectations of the culture, causes distress or problems functioning, and lasts over time."[40] Due to genetic predisposition, emotional trauma, and other factors, some people draw on a set of maladaptive behaviors to cope in life. With impulsive behavior, no real sense of self, persistent feelings of emptiness, unstable relationships, and a lack of empathy for others—particularly for her mother, grandmother, and best friend—Sula shows signs of having a personality disorder. Most notably, she displays traits of borderline, antisocial, and narcissistic personality disorders, symptoms that result in the Bottom residents characterizing her as a witch. Had she channeled her longing for fulfillment into some form of creativity, the narrator suggests, her life might have been different: "In a way, her strangeness, her naivete, her craving for the other half of her equation was the consequence of an idle imagination. Had she paints, or clay, or knew the discipline of the dance, or the strings; had she anything to engage her tremendous curiosity and her gift for metaphor, she might have exchanged the restlessness and preoccupation with whim for an activity that provided her with all she yearned for. And like any artists with no art form, she became dangerous."[41]

In this passage, Morrison appears to be inserting herself as a role model of sorts for Sula. Like the character, Morrison left her Ohio community to attend college. And the moment she arrived at Howard University, she "was loose," she admitted in the documentary *Toni Morrison: The Pieces I Am*. "It was lovely, I loved it . . . I don't regret it."[42] But Morrison's life amounted to more than sexual promiscuity and broken relationships, for she had the arts—drama and literature—to ground her. Discussing the meaning of her life, a dying Sula tells Nel that she has her mind and a loneliness of her own making, which she considers an achievement. But to Nel, and ostensibly to the reader, her life seems to be as empty as she feels inside.

Sula isn't the only individual in the novel whose life is her own. Ajax, a local man for whom Sula develops real feelings, grew up with an "evil conjure woman" of a mother.[43] He is drawn to Sula precisely because both her elusiveness and her indifference to "established habits of behavior" remind him of his mother, but he discovers the two women aren't the same.[44] As fervently as the Bottom women who attend Greater Saint Matthew's pursue God's redeeming grace, Ajax's unnamed mother devoted herself to folk magic, sending her seven children out to find the plants, hens, blood, herbs, oils, and other items she needed to practice hoodoo. With a keen awareness of "the weather, omens, the living, the dead, dreams and illnesses," she made an income from her knowledge.[45] Described as having no teeth and a hunchback, Ajax's mother recalls the archetype of the old haggard witch. Unlike Sula, though, she is a resource for her community with a craft that gives her direction in life. Having no interest in a career or a craft, let alone in her own identity, Sula begins to make Ajax her world and regard him as her possession. As if on cue, he leaves her.

In fact, Ajax's mother has more in common with Eva than she does with Sula, who has been accused of witchcraft but is actually devoid of all forms of magic. As a woman who has separated herself from the community, forced her grandmother out of her own home, and didn't intervene as her mother burned to death, Sula, much like Nel, did not learn how to examine life through an indigenous African spiritual lens. Her worldview is undercooked, and her capacity for magic remains untapped. Having developed their spiritual gifts and made themselves of use to their communities, Eva and Ajax's mother are the novel's true divine women.

The Need for a Scapegoat

Upon Sula's 1940 death—after which she somehow realizes didn't even hurt—the Bottomers celebrate, with only a few brave souls unafraid to "witness the burial of a witch."[46] But the young woman's death leaves a void in the community. While Sula was alive, women cherished their husbands and children for fear that she would one day take them away. After her death, the women don't relate to their families with the same sense of urgency. It turns out that the "evil" woman in their village had taught them to be good to one another. With their scapegoat out of the picture, they stop being as kind to their loved ones, and the breakdown of their relationships—accelerated by gentrification—marks the beginning of the Bottom's demise.

By 1965, Nel can hardly recognize the townspeople anymore because gentrification has transformed the community, but she has never forgotten Sula's grandmother Eva Peace—incredibly still alive, giving her a life span of biblical proportions. A visit to the old woman's nursing home rattles Nel, for Eva drops all pretense, demanding her to "tell [her] how [she] killed that little boy."[47] The narrator does not explain how Eva knows Nel was involved in Chicken Little's death, but the omission supports the idea that Eva's divine gift of sight allowed her to see what happened, even if she wasn't physically present during the tragedy (though the girls did see an unidentified figure in the distance when Chicken Little drowned). When Nel explains that Sula was the culprit, Eva quips, "What's the difference? You watched, didn't you? Me, I never would've watched."[48]

At first, Nel objects, insisting that Eva stop repeating lies about her, but after she leaves the nursing home, she admits to herself that she enjoyed seeing Chicken Little slip into the water. Sula was directly responsible for his drowning but was inconsolable afterward. "Why didn't I feel bad when it happened?" Nel asks. "How come it felt so good to see him fall?"[49]

The question brings to mind one Sula raised at the end of her life. She asked Nel why she was so certain that she'd been the good one and Sula had been the bad one. Like her mother, Helene, Nel had all the trappings of goodness. She was a virgin bride and a loving wife. Then after her husband abandoned her, she played the role of the wronged spouse and the sexless single mother who would only know the love of her children. Inside, she'd always been drawn to darkness because it made her feel alive, a contrast to the repression her mother had fostered in her from birth. Looking for a way out of the emptiness, Nel gravitated to Sula and found it thrilling to watch Chicken drown. While Sula relied on Nel to give her some semblance of an identity, Nel depended on Sula to make her feel something, anything other than the deadness she'd grown accustomed to in Helene Wright's household. In this way, Eva was correct: Nel and Sula were the same. They played their roles—the Blessed Mother and the disgraced Jezebel—as social norms dictated, but there was no fundamental difference in their character.

Nel finally arrives at this conclusion after she visits Eva. She realizes that she desperately misses Sula just as her fellow Bottomers feel a void without the dead woman's presence in their lives. The community needed an "evildoer" among them to remember to be good to one another, and Nel needed to learn to accept all parts of her personality—the virgin and the whore, the light and the darkness—to access her full humanity. In doing so, she makes a truly Christian choice. She steps out of the wronged-wife role and forgives her best friend, unleashing all the buried grief that decision entails.

Morrison's deconstruction of the virgin, whore, and witch archetypes in *Sula* allowed her to examine how sexuality is commonly used to declare women good or evil. But women's emotional complexity prevents them from fitting neatly into any of these roles. Those who are in touch with their divine femininity, like Eva Peace is, learn to integrate multiple facets of womanhood into their identities rather than compartmentalize aspects of themselves or ignore them altogether. Likewise, strong communities recognize the value in accepting the diverse personalities within them, even the problematic ones. The need to vilify another reveals more about the community members engaging in this behavior than it does about the actual scapegoat, a biblical symbol of a community's sin but not itself inherently evil.

5

The Folklore and Holy Women of
Song of Solomon and *Beloved*

Song of Solomon (1977) and *Beloved* (1987) debuted exactly a decade apart, with story lines and characters that, on the surface, don't appear to have much in common. *Song of Solomon* stands out as Toni Morrison's first book to center a male character, Macon "Milkman" Dead III, a restless young man who is unaware of his rich family history until a journey to find hidden treasure leads to his personal transformation. Inspired by a true story, *Beloved* explores the aftermath of an enslaved mother's horrific decision to slit her baby's throat to prevent the child from growing up in bondage. After Sethe Suggs kills Beloved, the child does not rest in peace. A ghostly Beloved—"full of a baby's venom"—torments Sethe and her remaining daughter, Denver.[1]

Although *Song of Solomon* and *Beloved* have entirely different plotlines, these novels share major similarities in their engagement of lore, trauma, and the divine feminine. Folklore not only plays an integral role in the two books; it also provides the foundation for their story arcs—both of which are linked to the trauma and legacy of slavery. In addition, holy women are central figures in each novel. While *The Bluest Eye* and *Sula* include churchgoing women, conjure women, medicine women, and clairvoyants, *Song of Solomon* and *Beloved* feature Black women preachers— Pilate Dead and Baby Suggs Holy, respectively—who are more adept at sharing God's word than the men in their communities.

This pair of prophetic female characters best supports the idea that an undercurrent of womanist Christology runs through Morrison's literature. For sure, her body of work includes Black women and girls who have been in some way victimized—abandoned or abused by the men in their lives—but her novels also feature women who are complete in spite of the marginalization and degradation they've endured. Pilate and Baby Suggs, for example, are spirit-filled women who do not view themselves as the world does. Certain of their inherent divinity, they love themselves—and, by extension, their Blackness. Preaching a gospel of love, these women draw on Christian Scriptures, their personal beliefs, and traditional African sensibilities to enlighten their families and communities.

While Pilate Dead is still very much connected to her African roots, her nephew, Milkman, has to leave home to discover why his heritage matters. In doing so, he learns that his great-grandfather Solomon flew back to Africa, escaping a life of enslavement but traumatizing the loved ones he left behind. The legend of the people who could fly isn't unique to Milkman's family; it is a real-life folktale passed down to generations of Black Americans to explain how enslaved Africans transcended their impossible circumstances. Concerned that young African Americans, like *Song of Solomon*'s protagonist, would become estranged from Black folklore, Morrison wove this legend into the novel. She insisted that the Black Americans who recalled a time when Africans could fly weren't just reciting a folktale but instead were sharing a legacy, as they really believed their ancestors had this extraordinary ability.

The People Who Could Fly

In 1935, when Toni Morrison was just a preschooler, President Franklin D. Roosevelt established the Works Progress Administration as part of his New Deal to help the United States economically recover from the Great Depression. Renamed the Works Projects Administration (WPA) four years later, the WPA put Americans to work building roads, bridges, schools, hospitals, and other infrastructure, but the endeavor also had an arts and culture component. Specifically, the WPA helped preserve African American culture by employing writers, such as Zora Neale Hurston, to conduct interviews and collect information about the

Black South. As part of this initiative, WPA workers spoke to formerly enslaved African Americans—some of whom were centenarians or had direct African parentage—about their lives, experiences, and traditions. In Georgia, the home of Morrison's paternal ancestors, workers with the WPA Writers' Project not only interviewed survivors of enslavement but documented slavery-era folklore as well. The federal agency's efforts marked one of the first times anyone had written down these myths, which had almost always been passed down orally. In 1940, an assortment of "flying African" folktales appeared in the book *Drums and Shadows: Survival Studies among the Georgia Coastal Negroes*, authored by the Savannah unit of the Georgia Writers' Project.

The book collection reveals that the myth about the enslaved Africans who flew away from the plantation and returned to their homeland varies from storyteller to story-teller; each version, however, has a common thread: a flight to freedom. In some retellings, a single person flies, while in others, married couples or even whole groups fly away by various means. Some flying Africans just lift themselves up, and others spin around before their departure or sprout wings. Some turn into birds shortly after takeoff or recite magical words in an African language to activate their flying abilities, but the brutality of the plantation overseer is often the catalyst for the flight. The storytellers also provide information about how the flying Africans became enslaved. The trickery and duplicity of white men typically explain how the flying Africans ended up in bondage and separated from their native land, for in many versions of the myth, a white man uses a red cloth to trick an African person onto a slave ship.

The different versions of the myth make it clear that flying is a special gift limited to select people, since sometimes parents can fly but children can't. According to the storytellers, magic determined which individuals could fly. Those who wanted to "take wing" had to believe in magic to activate their gift. On occasion, magical hoes, a representation of the backbreaking agricultural work enslaved Black people performed, appear in the "flying African" stories, but in other versions of these tales, the magic comes from within the person who takes flight, especially if the individual was African born. It was common for Black Americans to believe that Africans possessed supreme magical powers, as their spirituality and culture had been uncorrupted by white influences and oppression.[2] One storyteller, an octogenarian named Thomas Smith, told WPA workers in 1940 that God had given the African the same power He had given Moses when He allowed the prophet to change a staff into a snake. African heritage, then, was a source of pride for these Black Southerners; they believed that Africans were as spiritually powerful as the Israelites of the Old Testament. This flies in the face of the widespread assumption that enslaved African Americans were so psychologically damaged that they internalized white supremacy and shunned their African roots.

Precisely because Black Americans drew strength from their ancestors and native land, they circulated the "flying African" folktale in their families years before the WPA's efforts to record the myth. Typically, the elderly told the story to children to ensure that it would be passed on for generations. In her youth, Toni Morrison heard this legend numerous times. As an adult, she would read the different versions of the folktale the WPA collected and say the following about this mythology:

> The one thing you say about a myth is there's some truth in there no matter how bizarre they may seem. And the one that I had always heard that seemed like just a child's wish was the one about Black people, Black slaves, who came to the United States, and under certain circumstances, they would fly back to Africa. . . . I read a lot of those slave narratives—you know, that they published in the '30s—and the interviewer would ask certain basic questions, and then some others. He or she always asked that: "Have you ever heard of flying Africans or people taken up flying back to Africa?" And everybody said one of two things: "No, I never saw any, but I heard about it," or they said they had seen it.[3]

Well before Morrison wrote *Song of Solomon*—which connects the Black experience to the Bible, much like storyteller Thomas Smith did—she alluded to this myth in *Sula*. The character Ajax is obsessed with flight; he daydreams about airplanes, pilots, and blue sky, spending his free time "leaning against the barbed wire of airports" or "nosing around hangars."[4] Ajax is a prototype for *Song of Solomon*'s Milkman, who's also fascinated by flight, and Ajax's unnamed conjure mother is an early version of

Milkman's Aunt Pilate, a magical woman with a controversial name that's a homophone for *pilot*. In *Song of Solomon*, Morrison explores the truth of the "flying African" tale for the Dead family, particularly as it relates to the privileged and aimless Milkman Dead. Rather than simply repeating African American folklore in her works, Morrison illustrated how these legends were sources of racial uplift. They provided the Black community with folk heroes and a connection to Africa, and they also explained the fortitude Black Americans relied on to survive the horrors of slavery.

Reframing Black Mythology with the Divine Feminine

As the numerous versions of the myth make clear, not all Africans could fly. If all humans could "take wing" as effortlessly as birds do, the act wouldn't have become the subject of folklore. Tragically, *Song of Solomon*'s Robert Smith is not aware that only some Black people can fly in certain circumstances. So wearing blue silk wings, the insurance agent dives off the top of Mercy Hospital, convinced that he will fly across Lake Superior, but instead plummets to his death. During the spectacle, Pilate Dead sings lyrics that will play a pivotal role in the plot:

> *O Sugarman done fly*
> *O Sugarman done gone*
> *Sugarman cut across the sky.*
> *Sugarman gone home . . .*[5]

She tells her heavily pregnant sister-in-law Ruth Dead, who has just arrived at the hospital and is in the early stages of labor, that "a little bird'll be here with the morning."[6] Ruth responds that it's too soon for her child's arrival, but Pilate insists that Milkman's imminent birth is "right on time."[7] The next day, Ruth delivers Milkman, the first Black child born at Mercy Hospital. That Pilate is right about her nephew's arrival establishes that she has the gift of foresight, and her description of him as a "little bird" establishes that flight will play an important part in his life.

Although Milkman has the flying spirit, he loses all interest in life when he learns as a small boy that humans can't soar through the air like birds do. It doesn't help that his father, Macon Dead Jr., is as spiritually dead as his surname implies. Unlike his sister, Pilate, Macon values money and respectability over integrity and authenticity and teaches his children to do the same. In fact, Pilate's unconventional approach to life so appalls Macon that he cuts her out of his life and orders the rest of his household to follow suit.

The siblings might have diametrically opposed values, but trauma binds them together. As youth, Macon and Pilate witness white farmers kill their father, Macon I, to acquire his land. Morrison's own family history likely inspired this part of the Dead family history, since she once recalled that her father relocated from Georgia to Ohio after white men lynched two Black businessmen in his neighborhood. Although George Wofford never confirmed that he saw the lynching, Morrison believed that he had. She suspected that witnessing this act of violence fueled his lifelong hatred and mistrust of white people.

In contrast, seeing a group of white men kill his father does not lead Macon Jr. to hate a society that systematically devalues Black life. Following this horrific event, he adopts a materialistic mindset, believing his sister ran off with a stash of gold they found together when they fled home after their father's murder. Macon eventually accumulates his own wealth, but he oppresses his family to such a degree that he never truly enjoys his newfound affluence, and the coldness of the Dead household drives his son, Milkman, to leave his family behind. Milkman sets off to find the gold that Macon Jr. tells him Pilate hid long ago, but the treasure the young man eventually finds is more valuable than gold. He finds his rich family history and his self-identity—all thanks to Pilate, who has had his best interests in mind since he was in the womb.

Pilate not only predicts when Milkman will be born; she also sees to it that his birth will indeed take place, given Macon's violent opposition to having another child. After learning that Ruth is pregnant with Milkman, Macon tries to get her to abort by demanding that she drink half an ounce of castor oil. When that doesn't work, Macon orders his wife to sit on "a hot pot recently emptied of scalding water."[8] And when those methods fail, he gives Ruth a soapy enema and then a knitting needle to insert into her womb. Finally, Macon punches her in the stomach, an act of cruelty that sends his abused wife to seek out Pilate in desperation.

Pilate tells Ruth not to take any more of Macon's abuse and not to harm herself anymore. Described as a "natural healer," she gives Ruth advice about pregnancy cravings, telling her to eat whatever she wants—"crunchy things" like cornstarch, ice, and nuts—lest the baby arrive in the world hungry for the food denied to him in utero.[9] And using magic, she sees to it that Macon leaves Ruth alone. The narrator explains, "Years later Ruth learned that Pilate put a small doll on Macon's chair in his office. A male doll with a small painted chicken on its belly, Macon knocked it out of the chair and with a yardstick pushed it into the bathroom, where he doused it with alcohol and burned it. It took nine separate burnings before the fire got down to the straw and cotton ticking of its insides. But he must have remembered the round fire-red stomach, for he left Ruth alone after that."[10]

That it takes Macon multiple tries to successfully cremate the doll speaks to the might of Pilate's magic and the weakness of his. Pilate might share a name with the Roman official who ordered Jesus's crucifixion (her illiterate father liked how the name looked), but her good works and supernatural gifts make it clear that the Holy Spirit dwells within her. Her profession, winemaker, and the detail early on that she might make bread for dinner connect Pilate to Christ and the Eucharist. And when a preteen Milkman meets his aunt for the first time since his infancy, he finds her mesmerizing, similar to how Sula's Ajax regarded his conjure mother. Having intently listened to Pilate tell stories about the Dead family that his father never shared, Milkman for "the first time in his life . . . remembered being completely happy."[11] The smell of wine in Pilate's home intoxicates him, as does her singing and that of her daughter, Reba, and granddaughter, Hagar, who join her in reciting "O Sugarman."

Singing becomes a part of Pilate's life through supernatural means. Suffering from what might have been postpartum depression after Reba's birth, Pilate receives a visit from the spirit of her late father, Macon I. He tells her to sing, and she heeds his advice for the rest of her life. Having used *Song of Solomon* to re-create a story that's part of the African American oral tradition, Morrison engages the ears of readers by making singing a key part of the text.

When the spirit of Pilate's father visits her and not her brother, the novel establishes that she is "the chosen one" in her family. She will play a critical role in preserving her family history and ensuring that members of the next generation—namely, Milkman—pass on this information. By framing Pilate as a prophet, a role the Bible typically assigns to men, Morrison shows how women have long contributed to their families as seers and memory keepers. This was Morrison's experience in her own family, given her recollection that her mother, Ramah, received visitations from the dead. And like Pilate, Ramah had a mesmerizing voice, according to Morrison.

Pilate's enchanting singing voice, visitations from the dead, and rejection of materialism highlight what a force she is spiritually, but her Christian attributes also include her kindness to others. She allows Ruth and Milkman to take refuge in her home despite her estrangement from them, and she exhibits love in the face of cruelty as well. When her brother criticizes her gender-nonconforming appearance with a series of questions—"Why can't you dress like a woman? What's that sailor's cap doing on your head? Don't you have stockings?"—Pilate answers in all sincerity, "I been worried sick about you, too, Macon."[12]

Pilate's Christlike character is also alluded to when Milkman defies Macon and visits his aunt for the first time. He observes that "she was anything but pretty," much like the Bible describes Jesus as having "no beauty." Throughout *Song of Solomon*, the narrator associates Pilate with biblical imagery such as fruit, trees, and snakes that evoke the Garden of Eden, but the book also portrays her as an otherworldly figure. She enters this world more like a Greek goddess than a mere mortal. Immediately after her mother dies during labor, baby Pilate, also presumed dead, births herself. Macon remembers, "The baby . . . inched its way headfirst out of a still, silent, cave of flesh, dragging her own cord, and her own afterbirth behind her. . . . Once the new baby's lifeline was cut, the cord stump shriveled, fell off, and left no trace of having ever existed, which, as a young boy, taking care of his baby sister, he [Macon] thought no more strange than a bald head. He was seventeen years old . . . when he learned that there was probably not another stomach like hers on earth."[13]

The midwife attending the birth is named Circe, the name of the Greek goddess in *The Odyssey* who initially uses her magical powers to stop Odysseus from going home. Conversely, *Song of Solomon*'s Circe helps the characters complete their journeys. This includes Pilate, who travels alone from place to place after her father's murder. During these travels, her absent navel leads the people she encounters along the way to treat her as someone other than human. She is "believed to have the power to step out of her skin, set a bush afire from yards, and turn a man into a ripe rutabaga—all on account of the fact that she had no navel."[14]

Some asked if her missing navel made her a mermaid, a creature of significance in West African spirituality, as the Orisha, or spirit, known as Yemaya is often depicted as a mermaid. More broadly, Mami Wata (Mammy Water) is a water spirit worshipped in western, central, and southern Africa and throughout the African diaspora. These spirits are associated with healing, fertility, snakes, and, on occasion, misfortune such as drowning deaths. Unkempt with no social status, Pilate is far from a revered figure in her community; she is an outcast much like Sula. The town women turn to countermagic—sweeping up her footsteps and putting mirrors on her door—to protect themselves from her, despite the fact that she never bothers anyone and helps all in need. Pilate may have few flaws, but like the very flawed Sula, she's perceived to be a witch.

As she does with Sula, Morrison uses witch imagery to describe Pilate. When Milkman visits Pilate, she wears a "long-sleeved, long-skirted black dress," much like a witch would. And "her hair was wrapped in black too."[15] Before Milkman and his friend Guitar decide to pay Pilate a visit, they are already "spellbound" by the stories they've heard about her. In a novel about the legend of flying Africans, Pilate is a legend in her own right, and her magic sets her apart from her community. Having disregarded the norms about how women should look and behave, Pilate is viewed as a witch because she dares to be independent and unconventional in a society that forbids women from being either.

Although she's a healer, Pilate cannot save one of the people she holds dearest—her granddaughter, Hagar. The young woman has had a decade-long relationship with her second cousin, Milkman, but he grows bored with her and ends the romance with a letter. Like Hagar of the Old Testament, Hagar Dead has been used for sex and discarded, and Milkman's rejection of her causes the emotionally fragile woman to spiral out of control. She tries to kill him six times in as many months and flies into a homicidal rage after seeing Milkman with a woman who looks nothing like her. Hagar is dark skinned with "heavy" hair, while the other woman is light skinned with "silky, copper colored hair."[16] Determined to win Milkman back, Hagar gets a makeover, but a rainstorm ruins her new look and causes her to feel more dejected than she had previously.

Pilate tries to make her granddaughter feel better, telling her that Milkman will come around and that "he don't know what he loves."[17] Her words fail to soothe her granddaughter, though, and a heartsick Hagar falls ill and dies of a broken heart. Morrison shed some light on why Hagar dies prematurely, while her grandmother and mother manage to survive their own personal setbacks and anguish. She remarked, "Hagar does not have what Pilate had, which was a dozen years of a nurturing, good relationship with men. Pilate had a father, and she had a brother, who loved her very much, and she could use the knowledge of that love for her life. Her daughter Reba had less of that, but she certainly has at least a perfunctory adoration or love of men which she does not put to good use. Hagar has even less because of the absence of any relationships with men in her life. She is weaker."[18]

During Hagar's funeral, the reader sees a different side of Pilate. She's not only a grieving grandmother; she's also a preacher determined to eulogize Hagar in a way that the ordained minister cannot. She begins her sermon with the word *mercy*, uttering it first as a statement and second as a question. Next, she sings the word for so long that it sounds like a sentence, and in the call-and-response tradition of the Black church, someone answers in a soprano tone: "I hear you."[19] Pilate then turns her attention to the congregation and repeats the phrase "my baby girl" to each of the mourners. After singing out her grief, she grows angry, declaring of her granddaughter, "And she was loved!"[20] Pilate's proclamation is a direct rebuke not to Milkman for rejecting Hagar but to society generally for making the young woman feel like she needed to be something other than herself to matter.

Pilate's impromptu sermon is one of the literary moments that scholars from Harvard Divinity School highlighted during their 2012 special event "Have Mercy: The Religious Dimensions of the Writings of Toni Morrison." Jay Williams, then a doctoral student in the study of religion at Harvard University's Graduate School of Arts and Sciences, said that at Hagar's funeral, Pilate rejects the Black church tradition that funerals are really homegoing celebrations. She ends her eulogy not in joy but in anger, and her message is more poignant than that of the ordained but emotionally distant minister. Williams describes Pilate as "filled with the spirit" and a "sister of subversion." Moreover, he explains, "Her words from the Lord are more prophetic yet more painful, so Pilate interrupts the preacher, and the sermon becomes the place of pain and passion, the site of struggle, the crucible of confrontation."[21] Women have historically been locked out of church leadership roles, but this scene indicates that divine Black women are more spiritually complex than the church patriarchs who craft eloquent sermons that lack heart because they don't have an emotional connection to their subjects.

Because Hagar's death happens while Milkman is on his quest for Pilate's gold, he doesn't immediately find out about her demise. During his journey, he discovers the story of his great-grandmother Ryna, who suffered a fate eerily similar to Hagar's. From a cousin aptly named Susan Byrd, he learns that his great-grandfather Solomon "was one of those flying African children."[22] But when Solomon leaves Ryna and their twenty-one children behind, she completely unravels in his absence. After her mental and emotional breakdown, she wails in a ditch that becomes known as Ryna's Gulch.

Learning that Solomon's abandonment traumatized Ryna helps Milkman understand how his rejection of Hagar has the same effect. No one tells him that his cousin has died of a broken heart, but he intuits that she's dead, and Pilate is directly responsible for inspiring him to piece his family history together in a way that gives him insight into his own behavior. He has heard Pilate sing some verses of "O Sugarman," which he believes is an old blues song, but when he travels to the Dead family hometown of Shalimar,

Virginia, and hears the local children sing it in full, he realizes the tune tells the story of his ancestors and his great-grandfather's magical flight back to Africa.

Milkman has long wanted to take flight to shirk the responsibilities and people he feels weigh him down in life, but learning that his ancestors suffered after Solomon left causes him to reassess his obligations to those who love him. Having heeded her father's advice that "you just can't fly on off and leave a body," Pilate doesn't need to have such an epiphany.[23] Although she travels to a series of towns after her father's killing, she decides to settle down and find her brother after Hagar's birth because she senses her grandchild needs family and stability. While men like Solomon and Milkman overlook the needs of their loved ones, Pilate sacrifices her natural inclination to fly for her family, or so it seems. As the novel concludes, the reader learns that this magical woman never needed to "take wing" to fly. When a gunshot meant for Milkman mortally wounds Pilate, it finally dawns on him that he loves his aunt because "without ever leaving the ground, she could fly."[24] This makes Pilate, not Solomon, the true folk hero of the story, and in recognition of the vital role she's played in the Dead family, Milkman changes the lyrics of "O Sugarman" to honor her. When his dying aunt asks him to sing for her, he responds:

Sugargirl don't leave me here
Cotton balls to choke me
Sugargirl don't leave me here
Bukra's arms to yoke me.[25]

As she lay dying, Pilate's one regret underscores how Christlike she is. She wishes that she'd known more people. "I would of loved 'em all," she says. "If I'd a knowed more, I would a loved more."[26] Soon after she expresses this regret and asks Milkman to watch over Reba, a bird flies off with her earring, a sacramental object made up of her late parents' belongings—her mother's snuffbox and the slip of paper her father meticulously inscribed with her name before her birth. In death, Pilate and her parents have wings, and their ascension to heaven signifies that this part of the Dead family story is over. Forever changed by his aunt's guidance, wisdom, and love, Milkman will determine what happens next, just as Morrison hoped that her Black readers would take ownership of their family and community legacies.

In *Beloved*, Morrison has a different focus. It is "not a story to pass on" but a story to forget. The novel explores how the horrors of the past persist in the present until one confronts them and moves forward in life.[27] Drawing on West African folklore and the Christian themes of resurrection and persecution, the book helps its protagonis t work her way through trauma.

Margaret Garner: A Life Remembered

Song and Solomon and *Tar Baby* are the Morrison novels most associated with folktales, for the legends that inspired them are among the most well known in African American culture. Although the events that unfold in *Beloved* draw on West African lore about "spirit children" who return from the dead and torment their parents, this legend is largely unfamiliar to American readers, who have often cited the true story that inspired *Beloved* while rarely mentioning mythology's likely role in the plot. But both the real life of Margaret Garner—the enslaved Black mother who killed her toddler to spare her from a life of bondage—and the lore about ghost children are equally important to consider when examining the novel. In many ways, *Beloved*'s popularity has turned Garner's tragic life into its own (cautionary) tale, with recent articles about the woman who inspired the novel aiming to uncover the human being behind the legend.

Born enslaved on June 4, 1833, a pregnant Garner ran away from the Maplewood plantation in Kentucky in 1856 with her husband, in-laws, four children, and other enslaved families. When they made it to neighboring Ohio, the party of seventeen split up, and several of them eventually escaped into Canada.[28] Garner and her family weren't among them. Instead, they took refuge in the home of a free Black man named Elijah Kite, who has been described as either her cousin or her uncle. When slave catchers and federal marshals showed up at Kite's house to return Garner and her family to bondage under the Fugitive Slave Law, she decided to take her children's lives and her own. She used a butcher knife to slash her two-year-old daughter's neck, but the authorities prevented her from killing her other children and taking her own life, as she had planned.

John Jolliffe, the abolitionist attorney who represented Garner, sought to have his client tried for murder, which would have established a civil rights precedent by acknowledging that she and her daughter were human beings, but Garner was ultimately charged for property damage. During the two-week trial, abolitionist Lucy Stone took the witness stand and revealed that Garner said that she'd been sexually assaulted by her enslaver, A. K. Gaines, who had reportedly fathered two of her children. Stone told the courtroom, "The faded faces of the Negro children tell too plainly to what degradation the female slaves submit. Rather than give her daughter to that life, she killed it. If in her deep maternal love, she felt the impulse to send her child back to God, to save it from coming woe, who shall say she had no right not to do so?"[29]

Described as a "mulatto," Garner herself was reportedly conceived through the rape of her enslaved Black mother by the white man who held her in bondage. After Garner's trial, one of the longest involving the Fugitive Slave Law, Gaines sold her, her children, and her husband to his brother in Louisiana. During the journey south, the ship overturned, causing her baby daughter to drown. Garner is said to have been pleased that the accident occurred, as she didn't want any of her children to experience the degradation and sexual abuse she had while enslaved. In 1858, Garner contracted typhoid fever and died, but she has never been forgotten. Poets, writers, artists, and musicians have memorialized her in their work.

In 1859, Frances Harper made Garner's life story the subject of her poem "Slave Mother: A Tale of Ohio." Eight years later, Kentucky painter Thomas Satterwhite Noble made her the heroine of his painting *The Modern Medea*, in which he juxtaposes Garner with Medea, the Greek mythological figure who kills her children after her husband rejects her for another woman. In 2005, the opera *Margaret Garner*, a collaboration between the Michigan Opera Theatre, Cincinnati Opera, and the Opera Company, made its debut. Having won the Pulitzer Prize for humanizing a Garner-like character in *Beloved*, Morrison wrote the libretto for the opera, and in 2010, she told NPR what made this desperate mother's story so compelling. "The interest is not the fact of slavery," she said. "The interest is what happens internally, emotionally, psychologically, when you are in fact enslaved and what you do in order to transcend that circumstance. That really is what Margaret Garner reveals."[30]

The fact that Garner escaped to Ohio probably also interested Morrison in the enslaved woman's story. Never one to just repeat facts in her fiction, Morrison used *Beloved* to infuse West African folklore in the tale of an enslaved mother who killed her child to protect her from servitude. In her hands, Garner's story became a full-blown ghost story, only one much more heartbreaking than those Morrison heard as a child. She repurposed her family tradition of telling ghost stories to explore the institution that uniquely haunts US society, and to do so, she drew on a concept widely known in West Africa—the spirit child.

Beloved as Abiku

The simplest understanding of the children the Yoruba people call *abiku* (the Igbo call them *ogbanje*) is that these youth are "born to die," a transition they make before puberty, according to the lore about them. In addition to having short life spans, these little ones are capable of being reborn to the same mother multiple times. Because they die so young, only to be born and die again, their many nicknames include the Yoruba word *Apara*, which means "comes and goes." But each time they come and go, they cause their parents tremendous pain, an experience Sethe has when her daughter Beloved is reborn and terrorizes her after an initially joyous reunion.

Beloved is not born to die because she's an evil spirit, as the abiku are believed to be; she's born to die because slavery has made it impossible for a child like her to thrive. Beloved's return, then, is not an indictment of her mother for killing her but an indictment of the twin evils of slavery and imperialism that compelled Sethe to slash her throat to spare her from the brutality of bondage. But Beloved's rebirth also symbolizes how the Middle Passage—referenced in the book's "sixty million and more" epigraph—separated African Americans from their cultures of origin. As the novel unfolds, it's clear that this ghost child's reappearance is not just a reminder of the cruelty of slavery; it is a reminder of what Black Americans lost when they were forced to cross the Atlantic. When Beloved arrives, Sethe remembers both the trauma of killing her and the trauma of being removed from her ancestral homeland.

Altogether, the novel is a work of ancestor worship, as it honors the Africans who survived (and didn't survive) the Middle Passage as well as their descendants. In her book *New Black Feminist Criticism, 1985–2000*, the late scholar Barbara Christian discussed both *Beloved* and the Middle Passage, arguing of the latter,

It is the 400-year Holocaust that wrenched tens of millions of Africans from their mother, their biological mothers as well as their motherland, in a disorganized and unimaginably monstrous fashion. Yet for reasons having as much to do with the inability on the part of America to acknowledge that it is capable of having generated such a Holocaust, as well as with the horror that such a memory calls up for African Americans themselves, the Middle Passage has practically disappeared from American cultural memory. What did, what does that wrenching mean, not only then, but now? That is the question quivering throughout this novel. . . . How are African Americans recovering from this monumental collective psychic rupture?[31]

In psychological terms, this collective psychic rupture is known as attachment trauma, which refers to harm such as abuse, neglect, abandonment, or separation that disrupts a small child's ability to bond with a primary caregiver. The experience can adversely affect one's emotional well-being for life unless the trauma is addressed. For African Americans separated from their mothers and their motherland, attachment trauma became a generational phenomenon that scholar Joy DeGruy describes as post-traumatic slave syndrome in her 2005 theoretical work of the same name.

Since *Beloved* is, in part, a novel about the attachment trauma facilitated by the displacement and enslavement of African peoples, Christian contended that critics should consider how African belief systems influence the text. Recognizing the character of Beloved as a spirit child is one such way to make this connection. While it's doubtful that Morrison heard about this West African concept during her girlhood as she did the tales about flying Africans and tar babies, her exposure to West African literature in adulthood likely familiarized her with the abiku belief. Morrison recalled on more than one occasion that before her own career as a novelist took off, she discovered a New York City bookshop that specialized in the works of African writers like Chinua Achebe and Wole Soyinka, both of whom wrote about spirit children in their literature. In fact, Soyinka has a poem called "Abiku" specifically devoted to these apparitions. Not only did Morrison admire both Achebe and Soyinka, but she also called reading their literature an "education." During a 2014 celebration in Soyinka's honor, she said his works "really did affect [her] brain stem in the sense that you really don't see things the same."[32] She didn't elaborate on how her views changed, but having never traveled to Africa herself, Morrison's use of African mythology in her literature may stem, in part, from the "education" African writers gave her.

In turn, Morrison uses *Beloved* to educate the reader about the ancestral trauma that affects Sethe Suggs—and all people of African descent forced into the Americas. Throughout the novel, she provides multiple clues that the character of Beloved is a spirit child. For one, abiku have markings that identify them as reborn, and Beloved also has these markings, which are explained as the "fingernail prints" Sethe left on her forehead while killing her. Other than these lacerations, Beloved's body is pristine. She has not returned in the rotten corpse of a zombie, an undead figure also linked to the African diaspora, particularly Haiti, where such folklore dates back to at least the seventeenth century. Additionally, the argument that Beloved is an abiku gets a boost from the description of her as a "baby ghost [who] came back evil," since these spirit children have traditionally been described as evil, even inhabiting an "evil forest" in death.

In her 2019 article "Life after Trauma: Spirit Children in Fictions of the African Diaspora (Part 2): Toni Morrison's *Beloved*," Jessica Newgas points out that Morrison's characterization of Beloved mirrors Soyinka's description of an abiku. Beloved fights with Sethe, eats so much food in the house that Sethe goes hungry, plays with her so much that Sethe loses her job, and generally takes "the best of everything."[33] Still, Sethe does not discipline Beloved or order her to be obedient. Similarly, Soyinka described how the parents of an abiku "dared not scold her for long or earnestly" because they did not want the child to go.[34] Abiku reveal how the abandonment fears of childhood linger on well into adulthood. Terrified of losing their children once more and reliving the trauma that loss entails, the parents of abiku allow themselves to be controlled by these spirit children.

Beloved wields even more power over Sethe than a typical abiku because she reappears not as a baby but as the age she would've been had she grown to maturity. With a toddler's temperament and a woman's body, she mirrors how real-life people experience arrested development following early childhood trauma. While their bodies mature, these individuals emotionally remain the same age they were when their psyches suffered an irreversible blow.

Psychologically children, they are hidden threats to those who believe them capable of acting like mature and reasonable adults. Beloved's parasitic grip on Sethe, for example, begins to physically wear her down and endanger her life. This impossible situation requires Sethe's living daughter, Denver, and the women of the community to intervene, but Beloved's rebirth isn't solely negative; it provides an avenue for Sethe to work through the trauma of being separated from her motherland.

Beloved asks Sethe a list of questions that make her mother remember not only who she is but also her connection to (and separation from) Africa. The ghost child wants to know where Sethe's diamond earrings and intricate hairstyles are, inquiries that lead Sethe to remember the mark of the circled cross on her own mother, who was later hanged. As Newgas explains,

> The circled cross, in fact, originates from Kongo and "became the signage under which the creolizing of West and Central African traditional religions occurred in Haiti's Vodoun" in order to preserve "African peoples' beliefs . . . in the Western Hemisphere." Therefore, the thing that Sethe remembers behind the symbol is likely its original meaning as an ancestral cosmogram denoting her African heritage. In addition, there is the slap Sethe earned from her mother by asking for her own mark. The violence denotes the new meaning of the symbol that has displaced its former religious significance and indicates that Sethe is also remembering the ancestral trauma resulting from such displacement.[35]

As well as the circled cross, Sethe recalls Nan, the woman who nursed her as a child and traveled with her mother through the Middle Passage, for the pair were "together from the sea." Sethe also remembers that Nan spoke a language, for certain an African one, that Sethe can no longer recollect. Until her traumatized spirit child, Beloved, resurfaces, Sethe overlooks the ancestral trauma that haunts her and every Black American. Her mother-in-law, Baby Suggs, suggests that haunting is a universal experience for diasporic Africans when Sethe considers moving away from their home at 124 Bluestone Road (which some scholars link to Psalm 124) to escape Beloved. "What'd be the point?" Baby Suggs retorts. "Not a house in the country ain't packed to its rafters with some dead Negro's grief. We lucky this ghost is a baby."[36] She goes on to share how she has been separated from eight of her children, whom she suspects are now "worrying somebody's house into evil." Having suffered attachment trauma in life that persists in death, Black Americans have the unique experience of haunting and being haunted.

By haunting her mother, Beloved makes Sethe aware of the attachment trauma she's suffered because of her displacement from her motherland. This recognition allows Sethe to make sense of her past, who she is now, and how she can heal—a journey she embarks on once she rejoins her community. During her time of crisis, thirty village women come to her home at 3 p.m. Friday (the time and day Jesus died) to help her leave Beloved in the past where she belongs. Like Pilate, they show up singing, surprised that the "devil-child" Beloved does not actually frighten them. But as Baby Suggs asserts at the start of the novel (echoing Morrison's own words), Black people are accustomed to ghosts.

The Beloved they encounter has "vines of hair" and a pregnant belly, and after she leaves 124 Bluestone for good, a little boy searching for bait by the stream spots her "cutting through the woods, a naked woman with fish for hair."[37] The description of her as pregnant, near the water, and with "vines of hair" or "fish for hair" conjure up the Orisha Yemaya once again in Morrison's work. Yemaya is associated with fertility, water, and all sea life, and as a direct descendant of an African who endured the Middle Passage, the sea holds particular significance for Sethe. The Atlantic is what joined Nan and her mother together and what separates the African from the African American. Beloved embodies the trauma borne by this displacement, but the sight of her "cutting through the woods" also conjures up the evil forest the abiku call home.

Down by the stream, Beloved's footprints "come and go, come and go," just as the abiku do, and the spirit child's permanent departure from 124 Bluestone Road signals that Sethe has been liberated.[38] She and the community forget Beloved "like a bad dream," because "remembering seemed unwise." While Milkman needs to remember his African American ancestors to live a purposeful life, Sethe and those who care about her are best served by learning what they can from the abiku who torments them and quickly moving on with their lives. A lesson in ancestral and attachment trauma, *Beloved* is "not a story to pass on," the narrator notes. It is not a story of transcendence by flight but a story of loss by sea. What *Beloved* does have in common with *Song of Solomon* is the presence of a woman folk hero. Just as Pilate emerges as a healer and preacher in the latter, Baby Suggs plays this role in the former.

A Theology of Love and Liberation

A life of enslavement busts Baby Suggs's "legs, back, head, eyes, hands, kidneys, womb, and tongue."[39] Like so many women in Morrison's fiction, she has been given the cross, but the persecution she's endured as an enslaved Black woman has not robbed her of her heart, which she immediately puts to work upon her arrival in Cincinnati as a free woman. With that organ alone, she tends to the spiritual, emotional, and physical needs of her charges.

Just as Pilate cares for her pregnant sister-in-law, Baby Suggs cares for her pregnant daughter-in-law, and both women exhibit a talent for words. Mainly a singer and storyteller, Pilate reveals at Hagar's funeral that she also has a capacity for preaching. Baby Suggs sings, but she's first and foremost a preacher—the spiritual leader that the men, women, and children in her community turn to for guidance. Her gender does not bar her from this leadership role because an African cosmology allows for both male and female divinity and spiritual authority. As an unchurched preacher and a Black woman who has experienced the trauma of being separated from all but one of her children, Baby Suggs helps her community work through their own pain as she spreads a message of love and liberation that does not strictly align with biblical teachings.

"She did not tell them to clean up their lives or to go and sin no more," the narrator explains. "She did not tell them they were the blessed of the earth, its inheriting meek or its glorybound pure. She told them that the only grace they could have was the grace they could imagine."[40] Most importantly, she tells the community to love each body part, especially their hearts, "for this is the prize." It's a sermon of radical acceptance for a group of people who've been dehumanized, denigrated, and systematically taught to detest themselves. To counteract the messaging of an anti-Black society that seeks to destroy their bodies and minds or exploit them for the purposes of capitalism, her people must adopt a spiritual practice rooted in self-love. The manner of her preaching shows how African Americans were never mere Christian converts. Instead, as historian Margaret Washington Creel argues, they "converted Christianity to their African world view, using the new religion to justify combating objective forces, to collectively perpetuate community-culture, and as an ideology of freedom."[41]

Baby Suggs delivers her sermons to the "AME's and Baptists, Holinesses and Sanctifieds, the Church of the Redeemer and the Redeemed," as well as in the space deep in the woods known as the Clearing.[42] That she preaches both behind church walls and in the secluded wilderness again reveals Baby Suggs's comfort with both Western Christianity and an African cosmology. She does not need a designated holy building to give her words power, and she trusts the wildlife to clear out a space in nature where her community can worship with abandon. There, the men, women, and children take turns dancing, crying, and laughing—learning to love the flesh that their oppressors loathe.

While Pilate wishes she could have loved more people, Baby Suggs aims to teach her community to reject the hatred of the oppressor and love themselves. Hagar does not learn how to cherish herself and dies from a broken heart, but Sethe receives this message and lives. She comes to recognize, "Freeing yourself was one thing; claiming ownership of that freed self was another."[43] Baby Suggs may be unchurched and uneducated, but she is keenly aware that her community requires a theology of love and liberation to heal themselves. In this way, she plays as important of a role in Sethe's recovery as Beloved does. The spirit child gets Sethe to wrestle with the trauma of enslavement and displacement, while Baby Suggs gives her an education in self-worth in the wake of these profound acts of atrocity.

Engaging folklore, holy women, and traumatic family histories, both *Song of Solomon* and *Beloved* chronicle the journeys their protagonists take to become whole. With the guidance of his aunt Pilate, Milkman Dead sets out on a journey that will transform him from a selfish and aimless young man into one with a sense of purpose informed by his ancestors' experiences with flight. By portraying Pilate as both a guide for Milkman and a prophet, Morrison subverts the religious and literary norms that have traditionally cast men in such roles. In *Beloved*, she goes on to use another woman prophet, Baby Suggs, who preaches a theology of love to help her community find emotional and spiritual freedom rather than physical freedom from slavery alone. But it takes a village—Suggs, Beloved, Denver, Paul D, and the townswomen—to set Sethe free from the mental chains of slavery. Still suffering from the effects of attachment trauma, amplified by her heart-wrenching decision to kill her daughter, Sethe must learn to love herself before she's destroyed.

6

Paradise's Black Madonna
and Afro-Catholicism

Toni Morrison's *Paradise* was the first book she published after winning the 1993 Nobel Prize in Literature for a body of work that "gives life to an essential aspect of American reality." This honor, along with the 1988 Pulitzer Prize for Fiction she won for *Beloved* and the 1977 National Book Critics Circle Award she won for *Song of Solomon*, cemented Morrison's status as one of the world's preeminent writers. But after *Paradise* debuted on Christmas Eve 1997, Morrison recognized that her many accolades wouldn't prevent critics and scholars from dismissing her seventh novel. After all, she said, the book is "about this unimportant intellectual topic, which is religion."[1]

Paradise takes place (mostly) in the 1960s and '70s in the fictional all-Black town of Ruby, Oklahoma, established by nine families who in 1890 went on to found yet another all-Black town—Haven, Oklahoma. Ninety miles away from any other municipality, Ruby is a seemingly Black utopia where there's no crime, drugs, death, or television, and women can take midnight strolls without fear of harm. But Ruby is far from perfect: families adhere to a narrow and dogmatic interpretation of Protestantism and maintain racial purity by coupling with only the darkest of African Americans, even if that means resorting to incest.

The townspeople's bigotry doesn't stop at colorism, for Ruby's male leaders develop an irrational hatred for the group of women who live in the "Convent" on the outskirts of their community. First an embezzler's mansion, which was then turned into a Catholic boarding school for Arapaho girls, the Convent has become an unofficial home for troubled and traumatized women—among them a sexually exploited former foster youth, a mother who leaves her infant twins to suffocate in a hot car, and a poor little rich girl who runs off with her high school janitor. In the care of the spiritually gifted Consolata Sosa, an informal reverend mother, the Convent women find empowerment. Suspecting them of everything from lesbianism to witchcraft, however, Ruby's men ambush the Convent women one day in 1976 to blot out the evil they claim they represent. "God at their side, the men take aim. For Ruby,"[2] the narrator states. By carrying out a massacre, the men introduce the sin and crime they detest in the outside world into their paradise.

"Good intentions are distorted in some way so that they become ungenerous," Morrison explained of the ambush. "Now the community becomes that terrible thing, the chosen people . . . chosen to exclude somebody else. The notion of paradise as exclusive is what troubles me."[3]

The idea to write *Paradise* came to her when she visited Brazil in the 1980s and heard a story, later proven false, about Black nuns who routinely took in abandoned children. Despite their good works, a group of men murdered them for practicing Candomblé, an Afro-Brazilian religion that blends Yoruba spirituality with Roman Catholicism. "I've since learned it never happened," Morrison told the *New York Times* in 1998. "But for me it was irrelevant. And it said much about institutional religion and uninstitutional religion, how close they are."[4]

The all-Black towns that free people of color established in states such as Oklahoma and Kansas during Reconstruction also influenced the book. In his 1998 review of *Paradise* for Salon, Brent Staples surmised that Morrison's Ohio upbringing exposed her to these settlements because one such town, Langston, Oklahoma, took its name from Ohio's first African American lawyer, John Mercer Langston—an Oberlin College graduate, Reconstruction congressman, and great-uncle of Harlem Renaissance writer Langston Hughes.[5] About two thousand African Americans settled in Langston, but the population dwindled when they ran out of money and could not otherwise earn a living. So the town's founders resettled in Guthrie, Oklahoma, just as the Haven residents relocate to Ruby in Morrison's novel. Infused with what one critic described as a "magico-Christian message,"

Paradise is hardly just historical fiction. The book opens with an epigraph quoting "The Thunder, Perfect Mind," a poem from the collection of early Christian and Gnostic texts found near the Egyptian town of Nag Hammadi in 1945. Sometimes labeled a Gnostic myth, the poem dates back to the second or third century and is told from the point of a view of a female deity. Historian Elaine Pagels, author of the *Gnostic Gospels*, has described the work as "strange" and "marvelous." She said,

> It speaks in the voice of a feminine divine power, but one that unites all opposites. One that is not only speaking in women, but also in all people. One that speaks not only in citizens, but aliens, it says, in the poor and in the rich. It's a poem which sees the radiance of the divine in all aspects of human life, from the sordidness of the slums of Cairo or Alexandria, as they would have been, to the people of great wealth, from men to women to slaves. In that poem, the divine appears in every, and the most unexpected, forms.[6]

Paradise revisits the themes of "The Thunder, Perfect Mind"—the unification of opposites, the divine feminine, and the presence of holiness in unexpected places—again and again. But as Morrison predicted, the book's focus on spirituality earned it some scathing reviews. Michiko Kakutani of the *New York Times* criticized the novel for its "gratuitous biblical allusions," which included "comparing the story of Ruby's founders to the story of the Holy Family, turned away from the inn."[7] Zoë Heller of the *London Review of Books* argued that the book's message wasn't morally ambiguous enough, noting that "at some point, all Morrison's major novels seem to lose patience with the finicky business of recording moral blur, choosing to swerve off into the realm of moral fable and preacherly uplift."[8] And in *Broken Estate*, his 1999 book of literary criticism, James Wood objected to the presence of magic in *Paradise* at all, "since fiction is itself a kind of magic."[9]

This criticism points to a fundamental misunderstanding of Morrison's literary influences and philosophy. While she would likely agree with Wood's assertion that fiction writing is a kind of magic, she did not include magic in her work as a literary device. Its presence in her fiction reflects a pan-African perspective in which the lines between the natural and supernatural worlds converge. The dead coexist with the living, signs foretell the future, and healing does not occur in a doctor's office. In short, Morrison did not feature magical realism in her literature as much as she did the reality of an indigenous African way of being. And in the mold of the Black oral tradition, her works have a moral core because African American storytellers serve primarily as teachers who impart life lessons to community members, particularly the young.

In her work, biblical allusions reflect the Scripture-laden speech of real-life Black Americans, who passed down Old Testament stories just as they did folklore about flying Africans. Having historically only the church as a refuge from an outside world bent on demeaning and destroying them, Black Americans have always identified with biblical figures, especially those who suffered injustice and ill treatment. This history, not gratuitousness, informed Morrison's decision to compare *Paradise*'s characters to those in the Bible—notably Eve, the Israelites, and the Holy Family. In "The Master's Tools: Morrison's *Paradise* and the Problem of Christianity," Shirley A. Stave argues,

> Morrison very consciously parallels the biblical exodus of the Israelites with the post-slavery wilderness wandering of a group of "eight-rock" families seeking to establish an all-Black community removed from the sites of the oppression. Specifically, the text mirrors the divine intervention central to the original exodus, in which Jahweh's chosen people are led by a cloud by day and a pillar of fire by night; here, the founding families are led to Haven by a mysterious small man visible only to the group's leader, his son, an occasional child. Summoned . . . through a night of prayer that recalls Christ's experience in Gethsemane, the mysterious figure arrives to the sound of thundering, earth-shaking footsteps . . . that reverberate again once the wanderers have arrived at their destination and the man vanishes.[10]

The story of Haven's founding takes on almost mythological status, but as the elders die, their descendants lack the same attachment to this narrative about divine intervention's role in the town. When the younger generation leaves Haven behind for Ruby, they depend not on God to see them through this transition but on themselves. Although Ruby has three churches, the town lacks Haven's spiritual foundation, a fact that reveals itself in both the desolateness of the soil there and the dangerous legalism of the leaders. This context is missing from Kakutani's complaint about gratuitous biblical allusions in the novel.

Morrison found some of the criticism of *Paradise* to be "deeply, deeply insulting" and even "badly written," but she did not take it personally.[11] She told Salon that critiques of African American and women's literature intrigued her and that significant progress needed to be made to improve responses to such fiction. "I'm not entangled at all in shaping my work according to other people's views of how I should have done it, how I succeeded at doing it," she said. "So, it [criticism] doesn't have that kind of effect on me at all. But I'm very interested in the responses in general. And there have been some very curious and interesting things in the reviews so far."[12]

Since the novel explores subject matter Morrison explored in her earlier works—magic, religion, and misogyny— some of the unflattering reviews *Paradise* received are particularly perplexing. With a nonlinear chronology, a glut of characters, and points of view that change as quickly as one paragraph to the next, *Paradise* is a difficult book for readers who don't give it their utmost attention, but it is also familiar territory for Morrison fans. With descriptions of the founding of not one but two towns and the backstory of the Convent, *Paradise* amplifies Morrison's trademark village literature. As she does in *Sula*, Morrison complicates the virgin-whore dichotomy, arguing that the archetypes are inextricable from one another. And she uses two healing women of color to share a revelation about Christianity that her previous novels never made completely explicit.

While *Paradise* doesn't condemn Christianity, it argues that for it to be a tool of liberation, it can't be a reproduction of white religion. It must recognize the cosmologies of people of color and the social conditions that fuel oppression; moreover, it must include the divine feminine. Practicing a rigid and closed form of Christianity, the men of Ruby just imitate their white oppressors, spreading the hatred and intolerance their ancestors fled when they founded Haven. Through the novel's pair of healers, Consolata Sosa and Lone DuPres, the reader learns that a different type of belief system—one that considers an individual's spiritual wisdom rather than religious orthodoxy alone—is necessary for communal transformation, healing, and fulfillment.

A Hero and a Healer: Lone DuPres

"They shoot the white girl first."[13]

This is the chilling first line of *Paradise*. The opening pages go on to describe how Ruby's patriarchs, convinced that they have every right to extinguish evil from their town, methodically hunt down the Convent women. As the men invade the premises, they are appalled to encounter artifacts related to goddess worship and the divine feminine. The feet of the bathtub aren't claws but mermaids—"their tails split wide open for the tub's security, their breasts arched for stability"—another Morrison reference to the Orisha Yemaya.[14] There is also evidence that the Convent women practice Candomblé, for the shooters see that "tiny men and women in white dresses and capes of blue and gold stand on little shelves cut into niches in the wall." Candles have burned before these "graven idols," and food and libations have apparently been offered to them as well. With no knowledge of African spirituality, the posse of men can't deduce that these objects have ties to Yoruba spirituality. Instead, they view the altars as "satanic" and further justification to annihilate the Convent's defenseless residents.

Their decision to annihilate evil signals that these men don't embody what Morrison deemed to be authentic Blackness. In *Sula*, for example, no one attempts to drive the perceived villainess out of the community after her callous disregard for others and the bad omens—a plague of robins—that accompany her return to town. Morrison argued that African Americans lack the inclination to destroy evil, which is why none of the *Sula* characters kill the woman they blame for their misfortunes. "They don't run it out of their neighborhoods, chop it up, or burn it up," Morrison said of the Black community's response to iniquity. "They don't have witch hangings. They accept it. It's almost like a fourth dimension in their lives. They have to protect themselves from evil, of course, but they don't have the puritanical thing which says, if you see a witch, then burn it."[15]

The Ruby men don't realize how their impulse to snuff out evil makes them like the white oppressors who inspired their ancestors to start their own town in the first place. They also don't realize that without the encouragement of Lone DuPres, the town root worker, midwife, and member of one of Ruby's founding families, the Convent women would not have practiced an African-based religion at all. A character who bears similarities to *The Bluest Eye*'s M'Dear,

Sula's Eva Peace, and *Beloved*'s Baby Suggs, Lone is the catalyst for much of the action in *Paradise* as well as the novel's moral compass. She distinguishes herself by noticing how spiritually gifted Consolata is and urging her to put her talents to use.

At first Consolata, the former foster child of a nun named Mary Magna, doesn't believe in magic. She tells Lone that the Catholic Church forbids such practices and the folk customs related to them. "Her safety did not lie in the fall of a broom or the droppings of a coyote," the narrator explains. "Her happiness was not increased or decreased by the sight of a malformed animal. She fancied no conversation with water. Nor did she believe that ordinary folk could or should interfere with natural consequences."[16]

In this way, Consolata holds a viewpoint similar to Ruby's leaders, who dismiss Black American attachment to the African continent as "some stupid devotion to a foreign country" and regard community members who make note of omens, such as the buzzards flying over town before a wedding, as "simpletons."[17] Ruby may be an all-Black town where dark skin is superior, but most ties to an African way of life have been severed. Even the enslavement of African Americans is viewed as an event that's firmly in the past and irrelevant to present-day life. Likewise, the townspeople don't regard civil rights attorney Thurgood Marshall, then known for the landmark 1954 desegregation case *Brown v. Board of Education*, as a hero but as a "stir-up Negro." But once the nearest hospital to Ruby integrates, the residents quickly abandon Lone DuPres to deliver their babies there. They overlook that she's a seasoned midwife, herbalist, and invested community member who can tend to both their physical and spiritual needs. This differs from the African Americans portrayed in *Sula* who have no illusions about the Black community's experiences in health care: "They did not believe doctors could heal—for them, none had ever done so."[18]

That the Ruby townspeople ignore the resident healer among them is another sign of their disconnection to African traditions and their unwitting veneration of white norms. But not everyone in Ruby adopts such a mentality, for a young pastor named Richard Misner does view Africa as his ancestral home and hopes to learn about Black life before enslavement. Misner also objects to the townspeople's complete lack of interest in greater society. "We live in the world. . . . The whole world," he says. "Separating us, isolating us—that's always been their weapon. Isolation kills generations. It has no future."[19]

Misner's religious philosophy allows for the inclusion of liberation theology, and it is the philosophy in *Paradise* that Morrison said most reflected her own sensibilities about "moral problems." The pastor has the difficult task of balancing the tenets of his religion with the fight for civil rights and the concerns of local youth who increasingly recognize the outside world's importance. When the men of Ruby massacre the Convent women, Misner is out of town, and it's clear that he never would have condoned such an act. Unlike the other town patriarchs, Misner does not scapegoat the women or regard them as threats that must be vanquished to preserve Ruby's integrity. His worldview distances him from the town's leaders, but his perspective on religion, racial uplift, and the larger society is more complex and, thus, more beneficial to the community than the old guard's narrow line of thinking.

The rigid religious ideology that dominates Ruby life isn't the only source of oppression in *Paradise*. Seventeen miles away from Ruby, the Convent historically served as a place where Catholic nuns imposed Western Christianity onto youth of color, forcing them to sever ties with their Indigenous heritage. Back when the Convent was an Indian boarding school, the nuns taught Arapaho girls how to forget their Native cultures and identities, and Consolata came of age in the very same environment after Mary Magna kidnapped her and two other children sitting in "street garbage" in Brazil. Described as one of Ruby's "stolen babies," Lone was found as an infant by fifteen-year-old Fairy DuPres in similar circumstances. The teenager spotted her wearing a "filthy shift" outside of a sod house containing her mother's dead body. Baby Lone was "quiet as a rock," while nine-year-old Consolata's "docility" won her Mary Magna's affection. Both exemplify the "The Thunder, Perfect Mind" contention that divinity can be found anywhere, even in filthy little children.

The twin backstories of Lone and Consolata highlight how the women are spiritually connected—Lone intuits that Consolata has mystical powers because they are the same. Twins, both literal and figurative, speckle the pages of *Paradise*, with Lone chewing on Doublemint gum and Consolata feeling a magnetic attraction to a twin. Represented by the Orisha Ibeji and protected by the Orisha Shango, twins play an important role in West African culture. The Yoruba consider them to be magical, just as Lone and Consolata are. Because Fairy DuPres nurtures Lone's innate healing capacity by teaching her the art of midwifery, she grows up with an awareness of her magical abilities, an experience that largely eludes Consolata as a ward of the Catholic Church. Taught to view magic as evil, she hesitates to use her powers despite a mild interest in the subject and ancestral connection to the practice, but a self-assured Lone tells her that "sometimes folks need more" than institutional religion. They need to draw on the elements of nature, for God created them all. "You stuck on dividing Him from His works," Lone says. "Don't unbalance His world."[20]

When a Ruby youth has a terrible car accident, the life quickly draining out of him, Lone senses the calamity has occurred and orders Consolata to accompany her to the scene. There, Lone says that she's too old to revive the lifeless teenager but that Consolata has the power to save him. Concentrating on the blood streaming from his head, Consolata relives the accident, feeling the boy's truck flip over, his pain, and his "unwillingness to breathe." She then uses her power to resurrect him. "Inside the boy she saw a pinpoint of light receding," the narrator states. "Pulling up energy that felt like fear, she stared at it until it widened. Then more, more, so air could come seeping, at first, then rushing rushing in. Although it hurt like the devil to look at it, she concentrated as though the lungs in need were her own."[21] The teenager, who unbeknownst to Consolata is the son of her former lover, opens his eyes and sits up.

With some coaxing from Lone in a life-or-death situation, Consolata successfully performs the practice known in the book as "stepping in" or "seeing in" to rouse Scout Morgan. The character's ability to miraculously revive the dead teenager is related to the West African concept known as *asè* (pronounced "ah-shay")—described as the life force, energy, or power with which Olodumare, one of the manifestations of the Supreme Being in the Yoruba pantheon, imbues in all creation. With asè, one can bring about an event or effect change, as Consolata does at the scene of the car accident. Cut off from her Brazilian roots, Consolata feels equally exhilarated and ashamed to have tapped into this life force. The narrator never discloses her ethnic makeup, revealing that Consolata is nonwhite with green eyes, "tea-colored hair," and "smoky, sundown skin," a description indicating that she may be racially mixed, with the Indigenous, African, and European heritage common among Brazilians.[22] Although her childhood with a white nun mother figure taught her to distrust any practice removed from normative Catholicism, her ancestry equipped her to use asè to transform the circumstances around her.

In the end, Lone gives Consolata permission to use her power without shame. With a holistic view of spirituality, Lone considers Consolata's capacity to "step in" to be a divine gift and tells her that it's foolish to reject her God-given abilities. "God don't make mistakes," Lone says. "Despising His gift, now, that is a mistake."[23]

Consolata comes to heed Lone's advice and uses her spiritual gifts to empower the Convent women in her care, but this sets into motion the Ruby men's murder plot. "You think they got powers?" the men wonder. "I know they got powers. Question is whose power is stronger." After overhearing the men discussing their plans for an ambush, Lone has no doubt that her discovery of their intentions is an act of fate. She may not be a conventional Christian, but she believes that God orders her every step and makes His will clear to those who take the time to notice. Without once consulting God, the Ruby men determine who should live or die, but Lone doesn't make a move without first trying to ascertain God's will. She views God not as a mystery but as a being who wants people to play an active role in their destiny: "He did not thunder instructions or whisper messages into ears. Oh, no. He was a liberating God. A teacher who taught you how to learn, to see for yourself. His signs were clear, abundantly so, if you stopped steeping in vanity's sour juice and paid attention to His world. He wanted her to hear the men gathered at the Oven to decide and figure out how to run the Convent women off, and if He wanted her to witness that, He must also want her to do something about it."[24]

The first person Lone seeks out to stop the massacre is Richard Misner, her trust in him a testament to his character and an indication that his worldview aligns with her own to a degree. But he is out of town, and with no one else immediately available to help, Lone decides to intervene by herself. This courageous and righteous elderly woman believes that if it is God's will, nothing can stop her from foiling the massacre, but just as she has this thought, her car halts in a roadside ditch. Lone embarks on a hero's quest, but God did not intend for her to be the savior who prevented the Ruby men from gunning down the Convent women. It is His will for the tragedy to unfold.

Reclaiming the Black Madonna: Consolata Sosa

Toni Morrison claimed that she did not name her characters; they named themselves, but her novels are populated with figures—from Pecola Breedlove in *The Bluest Eye* to Consolata Sosa in *Paradise*—with deeply symbolic monikers. *Consolata* means consoler of the afflicted and is the name under which the Blessed Virgin is venerated in cities such as Turin, Italy, where the late Sister Consolata Betrone joined the Franciscan Capuchin order in 1930 and reportedly had interior locutions (private revelations) with Jesus. *Paradise*'s Consolata Sosa shares attributes with both the Virgin Mary and Sister Consolata Betrone. For example, before Consolata meets Convent newcomer Pallas, the teenager is so traumatized, she can't speak, but the youth miraculously finds her voice in the older woman's presence. As the narrator explains, "Connie was magic. She just stretched out her hand and Pallas went to her, sat on her lap, talk-crying at first, then just crying, while Connie said, 'Drink a little of this,' and 'What pretty earrings,' and 'Poor little one, poor, poor little one. They hurt my poor little one.'"[25]

Consolata is a natural at comforting hurt people, which is why the Convent becomes home to one victimized young woman after another. Although she has no children of her own and was unattended in Brazil's streets when Mary Magna kidnapped her, Consolata is also a natural nurturer. Her similarity to the Madonna is emphasized when Seneca, the Convent woman who introduces

Pallas to her, cannot see Consolata's face in the candlelight but recognizes "the Virgin Mary, the pair of shiny nun shoes, the rosary and, on the dresser, something taking root in water."[26] And like Our Lady of Sorrows, Consolata suffers from grief, using her pain to connect and empathize with other people in mourning. Consolata, however, soaks her grief in wine, her inebriation a state that would never be associated with the Madonna. There's also the fact that Seneca spots "something taking root in water" on Consolata's dresser. The phrase "taking root" calls to mind Lone DuPres's root work, an activity the church does not sanction, while the "water" alludes, once more, to the various water goddesses revered in Africa. Consolata certainly resembles the Virgin Mary in some ways, but she is also noticeably different.

The most fundamental way Consolata differs from Mary is that, having endured child rape before she became a ward of the Catholic Church, she's not a virgin. Thirty years later, she has a sexual affair with a married Ruby man named Deek Morgan. Her adulterous relationship and her alcoholism make her one of the "new and obscene breed of female[s]" that the town leaders want out. But as Consolata integrates her Catholicism with her ancestral spiritual practices, she rejects the Madonna-whore dichotomy and instructs the vulnerable younger women in her care to do the same. "Never break them in two," she says. "Never put one over the other. Eve is Mary's mother. Mary is the daughter of Eve."[27] A patriarchal reading of Christianity vilifies Eve while venerating Mary, but Consolata unifies these archetypes just as "The Thunder, Perfect Mind" joins opposites together. Consolata recognizes that she's both flesh and spirit and that her humanity allows her to transform the lives of women in pain. Having survived horrific childhood trauma and a broken heart in adulthood, she is not a pious figure who's separate from the hurting women who find their way to the Convent; she is the same.

A cook like Sister Consolata Betrone, Consolata Sosa consistently nurtures the women in her care by feeding them and teaching them to develop their own culinary skills. Consolata's food replenishes her charges physically as they recharge psychically, and the Convent grounds themselves have the distinction of being the only place in the Ruby area capable of growing the "hottest peppers in the world." In short, Consolata is magical, but the Convent is as well. As Rebecca G. Flores explains in "Black and Brown Goddesses: Feminist Iconography in Contemporary Chicana and African American Literature,"

> Ruby's inability to grow these coveted peppers further illustrates the barrenness of the town, and the fertility of the Convent. While the Convent boasts rich soil that yields strong roots, the roots are shallow in Ruby. In contrast to the Convent's abundance of fruits and vegetables, Ruby's "front yards were given over completely to flowers for no good reason except there was time in which to do it. The habit, the interest in cultivating plants that could not be eaten, spread and so did the ground surrendered to it." The gardens of Ruby, while beautiful, are superficial as they lack the nourishment and sustainability of the Convent's garden.[28]

Consolata's magic in the kitchen and garden doesn't reveal to her what a magical person she is. When Lone urges her to use her magic to resurrect Scout Morgan from the dead, she is conflicted, a feeling that intensifies when she uses her powers on a dying Mary Magna because she knows the nun would deem her abilities "evil." After she honors her mother figure and stops using her abilities to prolong her life, Consolata enters a deep depression known in Roman Catholicism as the "dark night of the soul" in which life appears to have lost its meaning. Tragedies, such as a loved one's death, can trigger it, but this state of being allows for a spiritual transformation, which Consolata experiences after despairing over the loss of Mary Magna. The attachment trauma activated by the death of her mother figure results in the death of Consolata's old self and "the birth of [her] true self."[29] This true self seeks her authentic spiritual heritage rather than the institutional religion that the nuns imposed on her.

As she decides to let go of normative Catholicism, she sees "the sky, in plumage now, gold and blue-green, strutting like requited love on the horizon."[30] The references to plumage and the colors gold and blue all invoke a Yoruba-based religion like Candomblé, for feathers are used in spiritual ceremonies and gold and blue are respectively associated with the Orishas Oshun and Yemaya, both mother goddesses. Consolata has lost her earthly maternal figure, but she sees her spiritual mothers on the horizon. Shortly afterward, she has an exchange with a mysterious man who shares her green eyes and tea-colored hair. She doesn't know him, but he knows her. The man's identity is never revealed, but scholars like Stave have speculated that he is the god-self to Consolata's goddess-self. He is a male god she can worship because he is a part of her.

Once she accepts all parts of her identity, she describes herself as Consolata Sosa for the first time, signifying that she's her own woman with her own history and not merely Mary Magna's ward. She accesses her ancestral knowledge, telling the Convent women, "I will teach you what you are hungry for."[31] She offers healing to her charges through the practice of Candomblé and storytelling about the (fictional) mother goddess Piedade, a name that means "mercy" or "compassion" in Portuguese.[32] The name likely also refers to Brazil's Church of Nossa Senhora de Piedade, home to a Yemaya statue. In Consolata's stories about Piedade, she fashions her own paradise, where "white sidewalks meet the sea," the cathedrals are scented and contain gods and goddesses, and Piedade sings but never says a word. In this vision of paradise, "organized religion and unorganized magic," as Morrison put it, come together.

Consolata's spiritual rebirth proves inspiring to the Convent women. They shave their heads, as initiates of Yoruba-based religions do, and release their trauma through artwork and exercises called "loud dreaming." Before long, the hurt, rage, and brokenness that previously ensnared them fall away. The women find peace, so much so that they don't recognize the Ruby men as threats. After rising to prepare their meals for the day, the group is caught off guard when the Ruby patriarchs invade their space to methodically execute them. But a curious thing happens after the shooting: no one—not Lone, not Richard Misner, nor anyone else—can find the women's bodies. It is unclear if the women actually died from their wounds or managed a miraculous escape, but *Paradise*'s ambiguous ending also leaves room for the possibility that God took these women directly to heaven as He did the Blessed Virgin during the Assumption of Mary. Unclear if the women are flesh or spirit, alive or dead, the reader sees each of Consolata's charges reunite with their estranged family members.

The last scene of *Paradise* shows Consolata with Piedade in a scene that re-creates Michelangelo's *Pietà* sculpture depicting a crucified Jesus stretched out on Mary's lap. Rather than a sorrowful portrayal of mother and child, *Paradise* closes with a hopeful image and one that reframes this holy pair as a Black Madonna and child. The narrator states,

In ocean hush a woman black as firewood is singing. Next to her is a younger woman whose head rests on the singing woman's lap. Ruined fingers troll the tea brown hair. All the colors of seashells—wheat, roses, pearl—fuse in the younger woman's face. Her emerald eyes adore the black face framed in cerulean blue. Around them on the beach, sea trash gleams. Discarded bottle caps sparkle near a broken sandal. A small dead radio plays the quiet surf.

There is nothing to beat this solace which is what Piedade's song is about, although the words evoke memories neither one has ever had: of reaching age in the company of the other; of speech shared and divided bread smoking from the fire; the unambivalent bliss of going home to be at home—the ease of coming back to love begun.[33]

Piedade watches another ship head to port with crew and passengers described as "lost and saved," "atremble," and "disconsolate." But she and Consolata will rest before completing the work they were created to do "down here in Paradise." The real paradise, then, is not in the heavens; it is not a clean aspirational place isolated from the rest of the world but one where all are included. Morrison posits that paradises have traditionally been described as male spaces with women framed as "interlopers," but a paradise based on exclusion is no paradise at all. This is why a Black Madonna and child occupy the utopia presented on the novel's final page. The "whole point" of her book, Morrison said, is "to get paradise off its pedestal."[34]

Paradise stands out as the Morrison novel that engages the divine feminine most overtly. It uses Lone DuPres, a woman already in touch with her spiritual gifts, as the catalyst that drives protagonist Consolata Sosa to step into her power. Once she does, Consolata draws on her ancestral religious heritage to spiritually restore herself and the women in her care. But fearful of the Afro-Catholicism in which the Convent women find refuge, the Protestant patriarchs decide to assassinate them. With this one horrific act, the men destroy the paradise created when their families abandoned the outside world, though a paradise where female divinity is viewed as threatening was never much of one. It is only after death that the Convent women find the peace and paradise that eluded them in life.

7

A Literary Legacy of Resilience

"**They're all beginning to** merge into one."[1]

Two years after the publication of her final novel and two years before her death, Toni Morrison made this observation about her books. It was 2017, and she'd gotten sidetracked, forgetting which of her eleven novels she'd been discussing and explaining to her interviewers that she regarded them largely as the same. While it's tempting to blame the memory lapse on Morrison's advanced age—she was then eighty-six—doing so overlooks that her books do read like volumes of one major work, dazzling pieces of tile, stone, and glass that together create an extraordinary mosaic.

Her last novel, *God Help the Child* (2015), was the book she couldn't recall; it tells the story of a little girl whose light-skinned parents loathe her blue-black skin. "It didn't take more than an hour after they pulled her out from between my legs to realize something was wrong," her mother recalls. "Really wrong. She was so black she scared me. Midnight black, Sudanese black." The child's skin color, her mother declares, "is a cross she will always carry."[2]

The baby girl grows up to become a beautiful cosmetics mogul under the mononym Bride, but she has some growing to do before she can succeed at a romantic relationship or recover from her traumatic childhood defined by an unloving mother, an absent father, and a sex abuse scandal. To get her mother's attention, the young Bride makes a false claim of sexual molestation against an innocent woman, resulting in the wrongful conviction and imprisonment of the accused. In the end, the ploy only wins the child some brief affection from her cold and distant caretaker, so disgusted by her daughter's complexion that she avoids touching her. Bride explains of her mother, "Distaste was all over her face when I was little and she had to bathe me. Rinse me, actually, after a halfhearted rub with a soapy washcloth. I used to pray she would slap my face or spank me just to feel her touch. I made little mistakes deliberately, but she had ways to punish me without touching the skin she hated—bed without supper, lock me in my room."[3]

The subject matter easily lends itself to the idea that, with this book, Morrison was revisiting another little Black girl, *The Bluest Eye*'s Pecola Breedlove. What might Pecola, tormented and rejected because of her skin tone, be like as an adult? By exploring colorism and child abuse, *God Help the Child* offers some clues about Morrison's first protagonist, not to mention some long-awaited redemption for her. While Pecola doesn't have a happy ending, Bride does—complete with a desired pregnancy and relationship. The book's "blunt moral," wrote artist Kara Walker in her *New York Times* review, is "What you do to children matters. And they might never forget."[4]

Pecola isn't the only early Morrison character the book calls to mind, as its focus on the beauty industry invokes *Tar Baby*'s Jadine Childs, a fashion model navigating a complicated romance and society as a Black woman. A novel that Morrison originally wanted to title the Wrath of Children, *God Help the Child* also includes the author's trademark magic, both in the form of an elderly wisewoman and in the fact that a romantic heartbreak sees Bride's body turn into a child's once more. Her breasts, pubic hair, and menstrual cycle disappear, a sign that she needs to tend to her inner child. It is the inverse of what happens to the ghostly woman-child Beloved, who grows to maturity despite her toddler death. In both cases, arrested development following childhood trauma is the root cause of these supernatural physical transformations. In addition, the novels address what writer Sarah Ladipo Manyika calls the "tension between memory and forgetting—forgetting as a way of overcoming."[5] In *Beloved*, the narrator asserts that the trauma enslaved people endured "was not a story to pass on," while *God Help the Child* notes that "memory is the worst thing about healing."[6]

And healing—through religious syncretism, racial pride, and the wisdom of elders—is the crux of Morrison's fiction.

Literature Defined by Trauma

From the beginning to the end of her career, Morrison never tired of exploring humanity's gravest sins—child abuse, slavery, racism, and misogyny—and their traumatic effect on African Americans. But her unceasing efforts to deconstruct these social ills in her fiction led to attacks on her writing. The late writer Stanley Crouch, a notorious Morrison critic, argued that she consistently set the Black experience "in the framework of collective tragedy" and would have been wise to tackle subject matter that reflected the world in which she lived rather than one filled with "endless Black victims."[7] Derisively referring to Morrison as a "literary conjure woman," Crouch argued that *Beloved* in particular belonged to a cultural movement with the following message: "Blessed are the victims, the new catechism taught, for their suffering has illuminated them, and they shall lead us to the light, even as they provide magnets for our guilt." He went on to argue that, from Morrison's work, "we learn little about the souls of human beings, we are only told what will happen if they are treated very badly."[8]

While Crouch's assessment of Morrison's work isn't altogether baseless, it is flawed. Certainly, all her books explore Black trauma, and it would've been instructive, even revolutionary, for her to present a fictional Black family that resembled her own. She grew up in a close-knit family with elders who shared their wisdom and worldview with her through songs, stories, and spirituality. They nourished her creativity, accepted her idiosyncrasies, and sacrificed to send her to college. No such nuclear family exists in Morrison's fiction, but you can find one in the literature of fellow Black Ohioan Mildred D. Taylor, known for her award-winning novels about the Logan family, which she heavily based on her own. Twelve years younger than Morrison, Taylor writes historical fiction for children and adults that illuminates the barbarism of slavery and segregation—and the power of African American resilience.

Morrison was not so different from Taylor, whose work also includes the healers, elders, and womanists found in her predecessor's literature. Black resilience interested both women, but instead of concentrating on African Americans who were already healthy, Morrison charted her characters' road to resilience. This pattern holds in nearly all her works. In *Song of Solomon*, a selfish and aimless Milkman must embark on a journey before finding fulfillment in the discovery of his rich family history. In *Paradise*, a lonely and brokenhearted Consolata Sosa experiences the dark night of the soul before using her spiritual gifts to heal herself and the women in her care. So while Morrison depicted trauma, she also depicted transformative healing, a characteristic of her work that Crouch conveniently omitted. Morrison intended not only for her characters to learn something about themselves but for her readers to as well. As she put it, "In order to get to a happy place—what I call happy, even though people are dropping dead all over my books—is the acquisition of knowledge. If you know something at the end that you didn't know before, it's almost wisdom. And if I can hit that chord, then everything else was worth it. Knowing something you didn't know before. Becoming something. There are certain patterns in the books and in life that look like they're going one way. And then something happens and people learn."[9]

Her fiction also features individuals who have already learned. They are not victims but survivors. Their faith in themselves and in God spares them from the brokenness of those who've taken cues about their self-worth from a society feminist bell hooks labels a "white supremacist capitalist patriarchy." As well versed in the Christian Scriptures as they are in African-based spirituality and wellness, Morrison's cast of elders provides the blueprint for what wholeness looks like for Black America. It is in these influential but nonlead characters that the reader can find shades of the family members who shaped Morrison's life. Her midwife great-grandmother, sought after for all sorts of medical advice, likely inspired characters such as Baby Suggs and Lone DuPres. Her storytelling grandfather can be found in *The Bluest Eye*'s Blue Jack, and her father in the patriarch of the same novel's Mac-Teer family. Morrison's mother is a strong presence in all her books, with every character who sings—from *Song of Solomon*'s Pilate to *Paradise*'s Piedade—reminiscent of Ramah Wofford.

Morrison didn't make these characters her protagonists, choosing instead to center those in crisis. This reflected her Christian ethos, for Jesus said, "They that are whole have no need of the physician, but they that are sick."[10] Morrison devoted her novels to the sickest characters because she adhered to the moral principle that "if you are free, you need to free somebody else."[11] As traumatized characters take center stage in her literature, the godly and magical Black women they encounter show them that an alternative way of life, one that allows for authenticity, is possible.

By placing these Black women storytellers, seers, healers, and root workers in pivotal roles in her "village literature," Morrison demonstrated that the African-based cultural practices they engaged in had real power too. Rather than silly superstitions, her books posit, these traditions have the capacity to heal, and the women facilitating the healing possess a divinity that generations of racial oppression couldn't shake. Drawing on West African cosmology and her own Catholic faith, Morrison depicted African American women as mother goddesses and Black Madonnas, iconography that feminist bell hooks argues the community sorely needs.

In the 2006 book *Homegrown: Engaged Cultural Criticism*, which hooks coauthored with artist Amalia Mesa-Bains, the scholar considers what it would take to reimagine "the Black female not as whore, bitch, bearer of violence, but as bearer of the sacred, the healing, the inspiring." hooks laments that "African Americans have not been interested in reclaiming representations of Black Madonnas."[12] It's highly plausible that many Black Americans don't know about the Black Madonna, since just 5 percent of this population identifies as Catholic compared to more than 70 percent who identify as Protestant, a denomination that does not revere Mary for birthing the Christ child.[13] In contrast, Mesa-Bains points out, heavily Catholic Mexican Americans have historically found solace in La Virgen de Guadalupe, whose dark skin is associated with Mexico's

Indigenous heritage and specifically with the ancient earth goddesses known as Tonantzin.

As a Black Catholic, Morrison distinguished herself by using her literature to reclaim the Black Madonna and Black female divinity. Her efforts in this realm are among the most overlooked of her literary legacy. In their headlines about her death, however, several Christian publications noted that she was Catholic, marking one of the rare times her religious faith received as much attention as her racial and gender identity. Morrison repeatedly emphasized that she was proud to be labeled a Black woman writer, but her religious background left as large of an imprint on her work as her race and sex did. On one hand, Morrison compared the victimization of Black girls and women to the persecution Jesus suffered, such as when Bride's mother says that dark skin "is a cross" her child "will always carry." On the other, Morrison suggested that Black women's aptitude for healing and fierce motherly love made them embodiments of the Dark Virgin. In particular, the detail that *Paradise*'s Piedade, a stand-in for the Blessed Mother, has skin as "black as firewood" breaks ground by framing Black women as holy, the source of magic and miracles.

Morrison's portrayal of the divine Black feminine is an act of resistance that counters the hateful representations of Black womanhood pervasive in society. "Where all women are objectified and hypersexualized . . . , Black women are far more often marked as hypersexual and subhuman," wrote Katie Edwards, director of the University of Sheffield's Institute for Interdisciplinary Biblical Studies, in the *Washington Post* in 2017. Casting Black women as divine subverts the dangerous characterizations that are all too often used to justify their abuse and mistreatment.[14]

The Morrison Effect

In the years after Morrison first introduced Piedade to readers, one of her most famous fans reclaimed the Black Madonna before an audience of millions. In 2013, singer Beyoncé, who has acknowledged Morrison as an inspiration, portrayed herself as the Virgin Mary in the video for her single "Mine." She re-created Michelangelo's marble sculpture *Pietà*, just as Morrison did in *Paradise*'s final scene. The superstar went on to use religious iconography in her 2016 pregnancy announcement and her 2017 birth announcement for her twins, Sir and Rumi. In both images, she stands in front of a flower wreath, a veil on her head and serenity on her countenance. In the pregnancy announcement, she clutches her exposed stomach, while in the birth announcement, she holds her babies against her breasts, her swollen navel peeking out beneath them. Although Beyoncé is largely unclothed in these photos, the similarities between these images and the classical depictions of the Madonna and child are unmistakable. Edwards argues that Beyoncé's reappropriation of the Virgin Mary constitutes a "biting critique" of the ideology that presents the divine feminine as an exclusively white domain. She asserts, "But Beyoncé doesn't simply create a powerful and iconic image of Black femininity in her pregnancy announcement images. Images of the Virgin Mary usually depict her fully clothed, including a head covering. The Virgin Mary's attire must suggest chastity, purity and (sexual and spiritual) virtue. Beyoncé also subverts this ideal by posing in mismatched lingerie, cradling her pregnant belly, and in doing so fuses elements of the 'Jezebel,' one of the most prominent stereotypes of Black women, with Virgin Mary imagery. This boldly challenges concepts of 'acceptable' female sexuality and racialized stereotypes."[15]

Well before Beyoncé fused the Virgin Mary and the Jezebel together, *Paradise*'s Consolata Sosa declared that these archetypes should not be separated, for "Eve is Mary's mother." After Morrison's August 2019 death, Beyoncé indicated that she'd read the book when she paid tribute to the writer by telling her to "rest in paradise." And in the vein of *Paradise*, Beyoncé has reclaimed not just Virgin Mary iconography but imagery related to the divine women of the Yoruba pantheon, particularly the mother goddess Oshun. She dressed up in head-to-toe gold, Oshun's signature color, in honor of the deity at the 2017 Grammy Awards. Two years later, the singer opened her Netflix documentary, *Homecoming: A Film by Beyoncé*, with a (slightly altered) quotation from Morrison's *Song of Solomon*: "If you can surrender to the air, you can ride it."[16]

Just a generation ago, it would've been hard to imagine an African American popstar reappropriating the Blessed Virgin, dressing up as an Orisha, and quoting a novel inspired by an African American folktale. In 1983, for instance, Morrison feared that younger African Americans weren't interested in passing down Black folklore, folk customs, or anything under the umbrella of magic or superstition. "They want to get as far as possible into the scientific world," she said. "It makes me wonder, in such cases, if the knowledge we ignore is discredited because we have discredited it."[17]

Buoyed by the student push for Black studies programs in the 1960s, a resurgence of Afrocentrism thirty years later worked to validate Black people's discredited knowledge. The Afrocentrism movement of the 1990s encouraged schools and educators to develop curricula with a focus on Africa, Africans, and African Americans. As theorist Molefi Kete Asante told the *New York Times* in 1991, Afrocentrism "means treating African people as subjects instead of objects, putting them in the middle of their own historical context as active human agents." In addition to educating Black students about the contributions their ancestors made to the world, Afrocentric curricula let youth know that the Black experience did not start with enslavement. Films such as Spike Lee's 1992 biopic *Malcolm X*, about the slain Black activist who sought to change the perception that "Africa is a jungle, of no value, of no consequence," helped broaden Afrocentrism's appeal. The movement also bled into music, with hip-hop group X-Clan and R & B artist Erykah Badu promoting Afrocentrism in their looks and lyrics.

The popularity Afrocentrism enjoyed in the 1990s can't be separated from the uptick of Black Americans in the twenty-first century embracing long-discredited folk and spiritual traditions. Interested in Black Southern, Kemetic, Haitian, and Yoruba cultures, to name a few, African Americans are training to be root workers, folk healers, astrologers, and priestesses, and some are even reclaiming once pejorative terms like witch to describe themselves. Of this phenomenon, largely driven by Black women, Yvonne P. Chireau, a professor and chair of the religion department at Swarthmore College, told NBC News, "Black women seem to have more of what I would call an orientation to the therapeutic, and that has been consistent. It's not just about women's power and witchcraft, and all these wonderful things that the white feminists were about. For almost every Black woman that I know who's involved in any of these traditions, it comes down to the purpose of this work is ultimately about healing—and not just bodies but healing spirits."[18]

The term *witch* appears routinely in Morrison's literature, most prominently in *Paradise*, where the Convent women are compared to a "coven." Her application of the term to women of color is as important as her reclamation of the Black Madonna, for generations of diasporic Africans have been branded witches for practicing their traditional forms of worship and healing. This history of persecution has largely been glossed over, with Tituba of the Salem witch trials standing out as the "Black witch" that looms largest in the American imagination. But scholars believe that Tituba was most likely of Indigenous descent and not of African origin, despite her portrayal as a Black woman in productions of Arthur Miller's *The Crucible*. During the Inquisition, however, enslaved Africans were tried for witchcraft in places such as Cartagena, Colombia. The Netflix series *Siempre Bruja* pays tribute to those persecuted for their spiritual and healing gifts and features a Black Madonna, the Virgin of Candelaria, to boot. The show premiered in 2019, with high anticipation from African American viewers, an indication of how much the community has evolved since Morrison expressed her concerns that Black people were discrediting their own African-based traditions.

Unlike *Song of Solomon*'s Milkman, who had to go on a quest to discover the richness of his heritage, young Black people today have already invested in the idea that an African cosmology has much to offer. While Toni Morrison isn't solely responsible for this trend, her efforts to exalt discredited knowledge are certainly a factor. On the day she died, one of the viral social media posts about her life and legacy included an image of her 1981 *Newsweek* cover. With her head slightly tilted and a faint smile on her face, she appears next to the headline "Black Magic."[19]

Notes

Chapter 1: Black, Christian, and Feminist: Toni Morrison's Village Literature

1 Hilton Als, "Toni Morrison and the Ghosts in the House," *New Yorker*, October 27, 2003, https://tinyurl .com/y5xnp72r.

2 Hermione Hoby, "Toni Morrison: 'I'm Writing for Black People . . . I Don't Have to Apologise,'" *Guardian*, April 25, 2015, https:// tinyurl.com/r6dmwhs.

3 Hoby.

4 Thomas LeClair, "The Language Must Not Sweat: A Conversation with Toni Morrison," in *Conversations with Toni Morrison*, ed. Danille Taylor-Guthrie (Jackson: University Press of Mississippi, 1994), 120.

5 Mel Watkins, "Talk with Toni Morrison," *New York Times*, September 11, 1977, https://tinyurl .com/f97yt5c.

6 Dick Russell, *Black Genius: Inspirational Portraits of African- American Leaders* (New York: Skyhorse, 2009), 231.

7 Sarah Ladipo Manyika and Mario Kaiser, "Toni Morrison in Conversation," *Granta*, June 29, 2017, https://granta.com/toni -morrison-conversation.

8 Nellie Y. McKay, "An Interview with Toni Morrison," in Taylor-Guthrie, *Conversations*, 153.

9 McKay, 153.

10 "James Baldwin: The Price of the Ticket," *American Masters*, PBS, November 29, 2006, https://tinyurl .com/yrawcmxa.

11 Michael Eric Dyson, "A President-Preacher from Anaphora to Epistrophe," *Sydney Morning Herald*,

January 19, 2009, https://tinyurl
.com/4cauxh6c.

12 Dyson.

13 Dyson.

14 Dyson.

15 Matthew 10:14.

16 Toni Morrison, *The Source of Self-Regard: Selected Essays, Speeches, and Meditations* (New York: Vintage International, 2020), 332.

17 David Masci, "5 Facts about the Religious Lives of African Americans," Pew Research Center, February 7, 2018, https://tinyurl.com/2ed6fkbs.

18 Charles Ruas, "Toni Morrison," in Taylor-Guthrie, *Conversations*, 97.

19 Robert Stepto, "Intimate Things in Place: A Conversation with Toni Morrison," in Taylor-Guthrie, *Conversations*, 17.

20 Dennis C. Dickerson, "Our History," African Methodist Episcopal Church, https://tinyurl.com/2srre9j4.

21 Dave Davies, "'I Regret Everything': Toni Morrison Looks Back on Her Personal Life," *Fresh Air*, NPR, January 22, 2016, https://tinyurl.com/3an4cyw3.

22 Davies.

23 Matthew 20:16 KJV.

24 Jacey Fortin, "James H. Cone, a Founder of Black Liberation Theology, Dies at 79," *New York Times*, April 29, 2018, https://tinyurl.com/bydejhwn.

25 Fortin.

26 Sharon Jessee, "The Female Revealer in *Beloved*, *Jazz*, and *Paradise*: Syncretic Spirituality in Toni Morrison's Trilogy," in *Toni Morrison and the Bible: Contested Intertextualities*, ed. Shirley A. Stave (New York: Peter Lang, 2006), 147.

27 "Obituary: Toni Morrison," BBC News, August 6, 2019, https://tinyurl.com/4225sd6x.

28 Alice Walker, *In Search of Our Mothers' Gardens: Womanist Prose* (New York: Harcourt, 1983).

29 Walker.

30 Walker.

31 Zia Jaffrey, "The Salon Interview—Toni Morrison," Salon, February 3, 1998, https://www.salon.com/1998/02/02/cov_si_02int.

32 Christopher Bollen, "Toni Morrison's Haunting Resonance," *Interview*, May 1, 2012, https://tinyurl.com/2zhpc8j3.

33 Morrison, "Memory, Creation, and Writing," in Morrison, *Source of Self-Regard*, 331.

34 Mark Mancini, "15 Fun Facts about *Dick and Jane*," *Mental Floss*, September 16, 2015, https://tinyurl.com/4hpvjuy3.

35 Toni Morrison, *The Bluest Eye* (New York: Holt McDougal, 1970).

36 Christopher Klein, "1929 Stock Market Crash: Did Panicked Investors Really Jump from Windows?," History.com, February 25, 2019, https://tinyurl.com/b4bnrvdj.

37 Joseph B. Treaster, "Zerna Sharp, 91, Dies in Indiana; Originated 'Dick and Jane' Texts," *New York Times*, June 19, 1981, https://tinyurl.com/ysb6y8cx.

38 Herbert C. Covey and Ira M. Schwartz, *African American Slave Medicine: Herbal and Non-herbal Treatments* (Lanham, MD: Lexington, 2007), 81.

39 Poonam Mahendra and Shradha Bisht, "*Ferula asafoetida*: Traditional Uses and Pharmacological Activity," *Pharmacognosy Review* 6, no. 12 (July–December 2012): 141–46.

40 Toni Morrison, *Playing in the Dark: Whiteness and the Literary Imagination* (New York: Vintage, 1992), 44.

41 Morrison, 44.

42 Morrison, *Bluest Eye*, 135.

43 Morrison, 136.

44 Morrison, 136.

45 Luke 2:10.

46 Morrison, *Bluest Eye*, 137.

47 Morrison, 143.

48 Morrison, 134.

49 1 Samuel 16:7.

50 Rondrea Danielle Mathis, "She Shall Not Be Moved: Black Women's Spiritual Practice in Toni Morrison's *The Bluest Eye*,

Beloved, Paradise, and Home," University of South Florida Scholar Commons, January 2015, https://tinyurl.com/7bwkefhk.

51 Mathis.

52 Harold Bloom, "Summary and

Analysis," in Toni Morrison's "The Bluest Eye," ed. Harold Bloom (New York: Bloom's Literary Criticism, 2010), 59.

53 "Summary and Analysis."

54 Acts 10:34 KJV.

Chapter 2: A Magical Black Heritage

1 Alison Flood, "Toni Morrison Cancels Memoir Contract Due to 'Not Interesting' Life," Guardian, March 16, 2012, https://tinyurl.com/yjwzj2u6.

2 Stephanie Li, Toni Morrison: A Biography (Santa Barbara, CA: ABC-Clio, 2010), 11.

3 David Streitfeld, "The Laureate's Life Song," Washington Post, October 8, 1993, https://tinyurl.com/2xayzncp.

4 Toni Morrison, "Nobel Prize Lecture," American RadioWorks, December 7, 1993, Stockholm, Sweden, https://tinyurl.com/vaxj5kd5.

5 Li, Toni Morrison, 9.

6 Toni Morrison, "The Black Experience; a Slow Walk of Trees (as Grandmother Would Say) Hopeless (as Grandfather Would Say)," New York Times, July 4, 1976, https://tinyurl.com/y3j9wrua.

7 Bonnie Angelo, "The Pain of Being Black: An Interview with Toni Morrison," in Taylor-Guthrie, Conversations, 255.

8 Angelo, 255.

9 Rachel Kaadzi Ghansah, "The Radical Vision of Toni Morrison," New York Times Magazine, April 8, 2015, https://tinyurl.com/4f7ubwpu.

10 Susanna Rustin, "Predicting the Past," Guardian, October 31, 2008, https://tinyurl.com/69x2z32t.

11 "TB in America: 1895–1954," American Experience, PBS, https://tinyurl.com/h9u85a4j.

12 "History of World TB Day," Centers for Disease Control and Prevention, December 12, 2016, https://tinyurl.com/32eatnsw.

13 Christina Davis, "An Interview with Toni Morrison," in Taylor-Guthrie, Conversations, 227.

14 Davis, 226.

15 Davis, 226.

16 Davis, 226.

17 Davis, 227.

18 Li, Toni Morrison, 5.

19 Li, 6.

20 Morrison, Bluest Eye, 133–34.

21 Morrison, 133.

22 Watkins, "Talk with Toni Morrison."

23 Davis, "Interview with Toni Morrison," 226.

24 Davis, 226.

25 "Magic Realism," Art Story, https://tinyurl.com/5b4ek42h.

26 Davis, "Interview with Toni Morrison," 226.

27 Anthony Chiorazzi, "The Spirituality of Africa," Harvard Gazette, October 6, 2015, https://tinyurl.com/93hvnhtm.

28 Davis, "Interview with Toni Morrison," 227.

29 LeClair, "Language Must Not Sweat," 122.

30 Joe Hagan, "Michael B. Jordan's Technicolor Dreams," Vanity Fair, October 2, 2018, https://tinyurl.com/3fu7yw95.

31 Margaret Busby, "Books: Toni Morrison: Beloved and All That Jazz: Margaret Busby on the New Nobel Laureate, Whose Wisdom Can Nourish Us All," Independent, October 8, 1993, https://tinyurl.com/p869wnw2.

32 McKay, "Interview with Toni Morrison," 153.

33 bell hooks, Yearning: Race, Gender, and Cultural Politics (New York: Routledge, 2014), 138.

179

34 "Josephine Baker and Her Danse
    Sauvage," Australian Ballet, August 6,
    2010, https://tinyurl.com/mxt532jm.

35 Nella Larsen, *Quicksand* (New York:
    Alfred A. Knopf, 1928), 59.

36 Tayannah Lee McQuillar, *The
    Hoodoo Tarot* (Rochester, VT:

    Destiny, 2020), 1–2.

37 Tony Kail, *A Secret History of
    Memphis Hoodoo* (Charleston, SC:
    History Press, 2017).

38 Kail.

39 Morrison, *Bluest Eye*, 165.

40 Kail, *Secret History*, 111.

Chapter 3: Black and Catholic: A Long Tradition

1   Patrick Giles, "Four Writers Forged
    by Their Catholic Faith," *Los Angeles
    Times*, August 24, 2003, https://
    tinyurl.com/4c8dtkcv.

2   Giles.

3   Nicholas Ripatrazone, email message
    to author, September 21, 2017.

4   Toni Morrison, *Toni Morrison:
    Conversations* (Jackson: University
    Press of Mississippi, 2008), 254.

5   Terry Gross, "'Fresh Air' Favorites:
    Toni Morrison," *Fresh Air*, NPR,
    January 2, 2020, https://tinyurl
    .com/mwk23x9h.

6   "Miracle of the Fish," Saint Anthony
    of Padua, https://tinyurl.com/
    xtm5z7a7.

7   "Miracle of the Fish."

8   "FAQs: St. Anthony Shrine,"
    St. Anthony Shrine, https://www
    .stanthony.org/faqs.

9   Manyika and Kaiser, "Toni
    Morrison."

10 Manyika and Kaiser.

11 Madeline Pecora Nugent,
    "St. Anthony and the Oppressed,"
    Messenger of St. Anthony, February 14,
    2003, https://tinyurl.com/
    3m4rxhjd.

12 Meredith Cash, "Late Author Toni
    Morrison Quotes on Writing, Love,
    Life, and Race That Show Why She
    Was So Beloved," *Insider*, August 6,
    2019, https://tinyurl.com/
    xtj3vm29.

13 Matthew J. Cressler, "The History
    of Black Catholics in America,"
    Smithsonian Magazine, June 7, 2018,
    https://tinyurl.com/wr6thh8a.

14 Emma Green, "There Are More
    Black Catholics in the U.S. Than
    Members of the A.M.E. Church,"
    Atlantic, November 5, 2017, https://
    tinyurl.com/28kepvcp.

15 Angelo, "Pain of Being Black," 255.

16 Cressler, "History."

17 Antonio Monda, *Do You Believe?
    Conversations on God and Religion*
    (New York: Vintage, 2007), 118.

18 Monda, 118.

19 Jessica Martínez and Gregory A.
    Smith, "How the Faithful Voted:
    A Preliminary 2016 Analysis," Pew
    Research Center, November 9, 2016,
    https://tinyurl.com/wsdhjxcn.

20 Toni Morrison, "Making America
    White Again," *New Yorker*,
    November 14, 2016, https://tinyurl
    .com/3nkk6b6n.

21 Morrison.

22 David Crary, "Black Catholics:
    Words Not Enough as Church
    Decries Racism," Associated Press,
    June 21, 2020, https://tinyurl.com/
    y3p7rdde.

23 Nicholas Ripatrazone, email message
    to author, September 21, 2017.

24 Monda, *Do You Believe?*, 117.

25 Davies, "'I Regret Everything.'"

26 Davies.

27 Nicole Winfield, "Pope Urges
    US Catholic Media to Work to
    Overcome Racism," Associated Press,
    June 30, 2020, https://tinyurl.com/
    2mt6e9ka.

28 Cindy Wooden, "Pope Reflects on
    Changed Attitudes toward Liberation
    Theology," Catholic News Service,

February 14, 2019, https://tinyurl
.com/baeka6np.

29 Wooden.

30 Damien Costello, "Pray with Our
Lady of Stono to Heal the Wounds of
Slavery," *U.S. Catholic*, September 1,
2020, https://tinyurl.com/2b8va7yp.

31 Costello.

32 Dennis Persica, "Oldest Parish Created
by African-Americans Celebrates
175 Years," *National Catholic Reporter*,
September 29, 2016, https://tinyurl
.com/nrat2a4p.

33 Morrison, *Bluest Eye*, 9.

34 Jon Lockett, "'A Miracle' Virgin Mary
Statue 'Cries Tears of Blood' Drawing
Crowds in Italy," *Sun*, August 7,
2020, https://tinyurl.com/jypuf54r.

35 Mathew Schmalz, "What Is
behind Belief in Weeping Virgin
Mary Statues," The Conversation,
July 23, 2018, https://tinyurl.com/
hdcnb4mt.

36 Davies, "'I Regret Everything.'"

37 "Church Custodian on Trial in Italy
for Weeping Statue Hoax," Catholic
News Agency, April 23, 2008,
https://tinyurl.com/y655nb4.

38 Lockett.

39 Watkins, "Talk with Toni Morrison."

40 Stephanie Paulsell, "Reading Toni
Morrison in Advent," *Christian
Century*, December 2, 2019, https://
tinyurl.com/93bdrm8.

41 Paulsell.

42 LeClair, "Language Must Not
Sweat," 122.

43 Cécile Fromont, *The Art of
Conversion: Christian Visual Culture
in the Kingdom of Kongo* (Chapel
Hill: University of North Carolina
Press, 2014), 27.

44 Emma George Ross, "African
Christianity in Kongo," Metropolitan
Museum of Art, October 2002,
https://tinyurl.com/2n9z2xae.

45 Michael Duricy, "Black Madonnas:
Origin, History, Controversy,"
University of Dayton, https://tinyurl
.com/8wxf4z49.

46 Song of Solomon 1:5 DRA.

47 Hannah Brockhaus, "Our Lady
of Częstochowa to Receive a New
Crown," Catholic News Agency,
July 27, 2017, https://tinyurl.com/
atnxh3n4.

48 Sonti Ramirez, "The Many Faces of
the Black Madonna of Częstochowa,"
Krakow Post, November 2, 2013,
https://tinyurl.com/2eb37r7z.

Chapter 4: *Sula*'s Deconstruction of the Madonna, the Whore, and the Witch

1 Orly Bareket and Rotem Kahalon,
"The Madonna-Whore Dichotomy:
Men Who Perceive Women's
Nurturance and Sexuality as
Mutually Exclusive Endorse
Patriarchy and Show Lower
Relationship Satisfaction," *Springer
Nature*, February 2, 2018, https://
tinyurl.com/ygq5tklv.

2 Danielle McGuire, "Opinion: It's
Time to Free Rosa Parks from the
Bus," CNN, December 1, 2012,
https://tinyurl.com/
y2e5zp8p.

3 Toni Morrison, *Sula* (New York:
Knopf, 1973), 17.

4 "Jezebel No. 1," Bible Gateway,
1988, https://tinyurl.com/cf2dv63t.

5 David Pilgrim, "The Tragic Mulatto
Myth," Jim Crow Museum of Racist
Memorabilia, https://tinyurl.com/
3yarsps9.

6 Laine Kaplan-Levenson, "TriPod
Mythbusters: Quadroon Balls and
Plaçage," New Orleans Public Radio,
September 22, 2016, https://tinyurl
.com/5cvb5mff.

7 Morrison, *Sula*, 18.

8 Morrison, 25.

9 Morrison, 26.

10 Morrison, 26.

11 Morrison, 29.

12 Morrison, 29.
13 Morrison, 29.
14 Morrison, 30–31.
15 Morrison, 53.
16 Morrison, 62.
17 Morrison, 65.
18 Morrison, 74.
19 Morrison, 74.
20 Morrison, 75.
21 Morrison, 78.
22 Morrison, 83.
23 2 Kings 9:22 KJV.
24 Morrison, *Sula*, 89.
25 Morrison, 90.
26 Morrison, 91.
27 Morrison, 92.
28 Morrison, 93.
29 Morrison, 94.
30 Morrison, 95.
31 Morrison, 113.
32 Morrison, 115.
33 Morrison, 114.

34 Morrison, 115.
35 Morrison, 117.
36 Morrison, 142.
37 Morrison, 143.
38 Morrison, 119.
39 Morrison, 119.
40 "What Are Personality Disorders?,"
    American Psychiatric Association,
    https://tinyurl.com/8dwuabmp.
41 Morrison, *Sula*, 121.
42 Soraya McDonald, "New
    Documentary Reminds Us That Even
    Toni Morrison Had to Fight Off the
    Haters," Undefeated, July 15, 2019,
    https://tinyurl.com/35w3x3dm.
43 Morrison, *Sula*, 126.
44 Morrison, 127.
45 Morrison, 126.
46 Morrison, 150.
47 Morrison, 168.
48 Morrison, 168.
49 Morrison, 170.

1   Toni Morrison, *Beloved* (New York:
    Vintage, 1987), 3.
2   Samantha R. Hunsicker, "Fly
    Away Home: Tracing the Flying
    African Folktale from Oral
    Literature to Verse and Prose,"
    Ball State University, April 2000,
    https://tinyurl.com/a4pv229d.
3   Sophia Nahli Allison, "Revisiting
    the Legend of Flying Africans," *New
    Yorker*, March 7, 2019, https://
    tinyurl.com/7xtjv3jf.
4   Morrison, *Sula*, 127.
5   Toni Morrison, *Song of Solomon*
    (New York: Vintage International,
    1977), 6.
6   Morrison, 9.
7   Morrison, 9.
8   Morrison, 131.
9   Morrison, 132.
10 Morrison, 132.
11 Morrison, 47.
12 Morrison, 20.
13 Morrison, 28.

14 Morrison, 94.
15 Morrison, 36.
16 Morrison, 127.
17 Morrison, 315.
18 McKay, "Interview with Toni
    Morrison," 144.
19 Morrison, *Song of Solomon*, 317.
20 Morrison, 319.
21 "Have Mercy: The Religious
    Dimensions of the Writings of Toni
    Morrison," Harvard Divinity School,
    2012, https://www.youtube.com/
    watch?v=5HxbrD8sQfI.
22 Morrison, *Song of Solomon*, 321.
23 Morrison, 147.
24 Morrison, 336.
25 Morrison, 336.
26 Morrison, 336.
27 Morrison, *Beloved*, 275.
28 Rebecca Carroll, "Margaret Garner,"
    New York Times, January 31, 2019,
    https://tinyurl.com/7y9bvunm.
29 Yolanda Pierce, *In My Grandmother's
    House: Black Women, Faith, and*

the Stories We Inherit (Minneapolis: Broadleaf, 2021), 28.

30 Bruce Scott, "A Mother's Desperate Act: 'Margaret Garner,'" NPR, November 19, 2010, https://tinyurl .com/yuuch9pn.

31 Barbara Christian, *New Black Feminist Criticism, 1985–2000* (Champaign: University of Illinois Press, 2007), 32.

32 "Nobel Laureates Honor Wole Soyinka," GBH Forum Network, 2014, YouTube video, 2:12:19, https://www.youtube.com/watch?v= F8-lURn9Ems.

33 Jessica Newgas, "Life after Trauma: Spirit Children in Fictions of the African Diaspora (Part 2): Toni Morrison's *Beloved*," Leeds African

Studies Bulletin, January 6, 2019, https://tinyurl.com/nffhbj72.

34 Chikwenye Okonjo Ogunyemi, *Africa Wo/Man Palava: The Nigerian Novel by Women* (Chicago: University of Chicago Press, 1996), 61.

35 Newgas, "Life after Trauma."

36 Morrison, *Beloved*, 5.

37 Morrison, 267.

38 Morrison, 275.

39 Morrison, 87.

40 Morrison, 88.

41 Judylyn S. Ryan, *Spirituality as Ideology in Black Women's Film and Literature* (Charlottesville: University of Virginia Press, 2005), 33.

42 Morrison, *Beloved*, 87.

43 Morrison, 95.

Chapter 6: *Paradise*'s Black Madonna and Afro-Catholicism

1 Jaffrey, "Salon Interview."

2 Toni Morrison, *Paradise* (New York: Knopf, 1997), 18.

3 Dan Cryer, "A 1998 Interview with Toni Morrison at Her SoHo Apartment," *Newsday*, January 19, 1998, https://tinyurl.com/ys9amwat.

4 Dinitia Smith, "Toni Morrison's Mix of Tragedy, Domesticity, and Folklore," *New York Times*, January 8, 1998, https://tinyurl.com/ 4k3vu5x7.

5 Brent Staples surmised Morrison's Ohio upbringing; Brent Staples, "Eden, Oklahoma: Trouble in Toni Morrison's Paradise," *Slate*, January 14, 1998, https://tinyurl.com/ 46cp5zhf.

6 "The Thunder, Perfect Mind," *Frontline*, PBS, https://tinyurl.com/ 5a3f325h.

7 Michiko Kakutani, "'Paradise': Worthy Women, Unredeemable Men," *New York Times*, January 6, 1998, https://tinyurl.com/bdujhusn.

8 Zoë Heller, "Feathered Wombs," *London Review of Books*, May 7, 1998.

9 Christopher Lehmann-Haupt, "Books of the Times: Faith and Freedom in the Magic Known as Fiction," *New York Times*, July 26, 1999, https://tinyurl.com/ 2sshvx8n.

10 Shirley A. Stave, "The Master's Tools: Morrison's *Paradise* and the Problem of Christianity," in *Toni Morrison and the Bible: Contested Intertextualities*, ed. Shirley A. Stave (New York: Peter Lang, 2006), 217.

11 Smith, "Toni Morrison's Mix."

12 Jaffrey, "Salon Interview."

13 Morrison, *Paradise*, 3.

14 Morrison, 9.

15 Black Creation Annual, "Conversations with Alice Childress and Toni Morrison," in Taylor-Guthrie, *Conversations*, 8.

16 Morrison, *Paradise*, 244.

17 Morrison, 210.

18 Morrison, *Sula*, 90.

19 Morrison, *Paradise*, 210.

20 Morrison, 244.

21 Morrison, 245.

22 Morrison, 223.

23 Morrison, 248.
24 Morrison, 273.
25 Morrison, 173.
26 Morrison, 172.
27 Morrison, 262.
28 Rebecca G. Flores, "Black and Brown Goddesses: Feminist Iconography in Contemporary Chicana and African American Literature," Texas State University, August 2010, https://tinyurl.com/23npckjm.

29 Eckhart Tolle, "Eckhart on the Dark Night of the Soul," https://tinyurl.com/8rad4zkr.
30 Morrison, *Paradise*, 251.
31 Morrison, 262.
32 Patricia Monaghan, *Goddesses in World Culture* (Santa Barbara, CA: ABC-Clio, 2010), 54.
33 Morrison, *Paradise*, 318.
34 Smith, "Toni Morrison's Mix."

Chapter 7: A Literary Legacy of Resilience

1 Manyika and Kaiser, "Toni Morrison."
2 Toni Morrison, *God Help the Child* (New York: Vintage, 2015), 50.
3 Morrison, 37.
4 Kara Walker, "Toni Morrison's 'God Help the Child,'" *New York Times*, April 19, 2015, https://tinyurl.com/29b4z2tc.
5 Manyika and Kaiser, "Toni Morrison."
6 Manyika and Kaiser.
7 Lily Rothman, "How Toni Morrison's New Novel Answers Her Critics," *Time*, April 21, 2015, https://time.com/3819769/toni-morrison-1998.
8 Stanley Crouch, "Literary Conjure Woman," *New Republic*, October 19, 1987, https://tinyurl.com/3cedannw.
9 Manyika and Kaiser, "Toni Morrison."
10 Mark 2:17 KJV.
11 Cash, "Late Author Toni Morrison."
12 Amalia Mesa-Bains and bell hooks, *Homegrown: Engaged Cultural Criticism* (New York: Taylor & Francis, 2017), 23.
13 "Black Americans Are More Likely to Be Christian Than Americans Overall," Pew Research Center, April 20, 2018, https://tinyurl.com/5bj9rwk9.
14 Katie Edwards, "Beyoncé's Virgin Mary Imagery Challenges Religious and Sexual Stereotypes," *Washington Post*, July 14, 2017, https://tinyurl.com/sjm8x93s.
15 Edwards, "Beyoncé's Virgin Mary Imagery Challenges Religious and Sexual Stereotypes."
16 Suyin Haynes, "From Nina Simone to Maya Angelou: How Beyoncé Honors 9 Black Icons in Her Homecoming Documentary," *Time*, April 17, 2019, https://tinyurl.com/xu628zf4.
17 McKay, "Interview with Toni Morrison," 154.
18 Nadra Nittle, "'We're Reclaiming These Traditions': Black Women Embrace the Spiritual Realm," NBC News, October 30, 2020, https://tinyurl.com/v5fbu65u.
19 Daniel Avery, "Revisiting Toni Morrison's 1981 Newsweek Cover Story: 'The Melting Pot Never Worked,'" *Newsweek*, August 6, 2019, https://tinyurl.com/rw76affm.

Index

colorism, 16, 142, 164

Cone, James H., 11, 12, 13

conjure, conjurers, 44, 45, 46, 47, 100, 104, 110, 114, 118, 166. *See also* root work, root workers

Convent, 51, 71, 142, 148–49, 151–52, 154–56, 158, 160, 162, 174

cosmology, 36, 48, 137, 169, 175

Covarrubias, Miguel, 44

Crane, Helga, 43

Crawford, Joan, 41

Creel, Margaret Washington, 138

Creole, 85, 88–89, 99

Cressler, Matthew, 60, 67

Crouch, Stanley, 166–67

Crucible, The (Miller), 174

Danse Sauvage, 42

Dark Virgin, 79, 80, 170. *See also* Black Madonna

Day, Dorothy, 49

Dead, Hagar, 119, 122, 123, 124, 125, 137, 139

Dead, Macon, I, 119

Dead, Macon, Jr., 116–20

Dead, Milkman, 109, 111, 114–26, 136, 139, 167, 175

Dead, Pilate, 61, 110–11, 115–26, 135, 137, 139, 168

Dead, Reba, 118, 119, 122, 126

Dead, Ruth, 116–19

de Bulhões, Fernando Martins. *See* Anthony of Padua, Saint

DeGruy, Joy, 131

Delilah, 34

Delille, Henriette, 71, 87

Demeter, 53

de Régnier, Pierre, 42

Dick and Jane, 16, 17, 19, 23

Dietrich, Marlene, 41

divine feminine, 9, 50, 53, 73, 79–80, 96, 99, 105–6, 108, 110, 115, 124, 144, 148, 154, 162, 170–72

Dostoevsky, Fyodor, 26

Douglas, Aaron, 44

DuBois, W. E. B., 40

DuPres, Fairy, 152–53

DuPres, Lone, 148–50, 152–55, 157, 159, 162, 168

Duricy, Michael, 79, 80

Dyson, Michael Eric, 6

Egypt, 7, 41, 56, 144

Ellison, Ralph, 1

Esteban the Moor. *See* Black Stephen

Eve, 83, 92, 157

feminist, feminism, 1, 13, 14, 15, 23, 41, 130, 158, 168, 169, 174. *See also* womanist(s), womanism

First Corinthians, 20, 53, 54

Flaubert, Gustave, 26

Flores, Angel, 36

Flores, Rebecca G., 158

Floyd, George, 65

Flying Africans, 112, 113, 114, 115, 121, 124, 132, 145

folk healers, 173

folk hero, 115, 125, 126, 129, 133, 137

folklore, folktales, 9, 16, 17, 23, 38, 39, 40, 41, 44, 77, 109, 110,